Self Love & Spiritua

Transform your mindset, strengthen your
self-worth and manifest the life you desire.

Dani Watson

ISBN: 9798621495848

Cover design by: Dani Watson

For Raffi,
My darling girl.

As I begin to write this book, you are just three months young with your whole life ahead of you. While I trust that your life will be blessed with so much love, incredible adventures, and amazing opportunities, there are a few things that I would like you to know.

Being a girl comes with a lot of expectations, but your priority should always be to love, honor, and respect yourself & your desires before you try to please anyone else.

The greatest love story you will ever have will be the one you have with yourself, so be kind to yourself. Be your own best friend and soulmate before you become anyone else's.

While I stand for Girl Power, I want you to know that It's ok to be vulnerable. It's ok, to be emotional, to cry, to sometimes feel like giving up. Being vulnerable is a strength, not a weakness.

You have the potential to become and create anything your heart desires. I want you to choose a path that lights you up, do what you love, do it with passion & do it to the best of your ability.

The world is such an incredible place, so make plenty of time for adventures, travel & new experiences. Collect memories over things.

Don't listen to anyone who tells you "you can't" or "that's not possible". You live in a world with so many opportunities and resources at your fingertips to make most dreams a reality. Prove them wrong.

Don't be afraid to make mistakes. You will fall. You will fail. Learn to embrace the journey, knowing that you are always divinely guided and that everything happens at the exact moment it is meant to.

Lastly, I want you to know that you are loved beyond measure & I can't wait to see you blossom into the strong, smart & inspiring woman I know you will one day become.

Love you always.

Mama.

Xx

The Truth About Self Love

To love oneself is the beginning of a lifelong romance
~ Oscar Wilde

Self Love is not just about taking a bubble bath or having a pampering session. Self Love is not about having a regular yoga practice or drinking herbal teas while cuddling up with an inspiring book. While all of these things are lovely, true Self Love goes much deeper than this.

True Self Love is about blossoming into the best possible version of you, the version that knows no limits to what she can achieve or who she can become.

True Self Love is not so much about what you do, but how you think and feel about yourself and the world around you.

True Self Love is about recognising where you are holding onto thoughts and beliefs that do not serve you and doing the inner work to change them.

True Self Love is about releasing negative energy, forgiving the past and raising your vibration, so that you feel amazing from the inside.

True Self Love is about allowing yourself to become the woman you are meant to be, and having the clarity and confidence to create the life you truly crave.

Once you cultivate true Self Love and rise up as the empowered goddess that you are, you will realise that you can be, do and have anything your heart desires.

Self Love & Spiritual Alchemy is a framework that will teach you how to transform your inner world and connect with the power of The Universe so that you can manifest a life that sets your soul on fire. Within the pages of this book, I want to share with you a step by step process which, if you commit to, will propel you into a life bigger than even your wildest dreams. Using this process, I've witnessed:

- Women who have been struggling with crushingly low self-worth transform into confident and empowered goddesses in a matter of weeks.
- Women that have manifested thousands of pounds from doing work that they are truly passionate about.

- Women who have manifested their soulmate after years of searching.
- Women who have seen their businesses take off after years of struggling.
- Women go from fears, doubts, and self-sabotage, to stepping into their power and attracting anything they desire with ease.

Now it's your turn.

With this book as your guide, I want to empower you to become the woman you are meant to be and to create the life that you want to live. When you start accepting that you are worthy of amazing things, start believing you are capable of achieving them, and start to truly love yourself, anything is possible.

This book is filled with practical exercises to support you on your quest for Self Love and manifesting the life you desire, but please make sure to also access the Self Love Club for free by visiting www.daniwatson.com/selfloveclub.

Within this free member's area, you will get access to downloadable versions of the exercises within this book plus guided meditations, video support, and other coaching tools to help you along the way.

Everyone within the Self Love Club will also receive an invite to join our free community so that you can connect with like-minded women who are ready to support you and lift you higher.

I'm so happy and grateful to be with you on this journey, and I'm so excited to see where this work takes you.

Lots of love and gratitude,

Dani

My Story

Turn Your Wounds to Wisdom ~ Oprah

We all have a story.

Mine starts where many tales of transformation and spiritual growth start, and that is at my Rock Bottom. Now I'd like to begin by saying that for anyone experiencing their Rock Bottom right now, I know it can feel like a shitty place to hang out.

When life fails to unfold as you hoped it would, when the career doesn't go as planned, or the relationship comes to an end, when you are struggling to make ends meet or to find the motivation to work out and eat healthily, when you are dealing with overwhelming amounts of stress or battling with anxiety, when you are feeling lost and unfulfilled, or your self-worth is at an all-time low, whatever it is you're going through know this:

Rock bottom can become the catalyst for building a beautiful new beginning and catapult your life forwards in ways you never even anticipated.

It was off the back of possibly the lowest period in my life that I discovered the world of Self Love, mindset and Law of Attraction, a world which I'm excited to invite you into within you in the pages of this book.

Without my Rock Bottom, I may not have discovered my spiritual path and, therefore, may not have had the opportunity to develop into the woman I am today and experience all the mind-blowing things I have since manifested.

But even if Rock Bottom isn't where you're at right now, if life is neither here nor there but just a little bit "meh," I want you to realize that this work still has the power to shake things up for you in more ways than you know.

And, if your life is already amazing, it's about to get even better. Before I share my story, I'd like to point out that my life may not have been at Rock Bottom in comparison to other people's standards. I was functioning. I was getting up and going to work. I would still go out and see friends (albeit drinking far too much), and I was exercising (albeit exercising far too much). While I did start to battle with anxiety and panic attacks, I certainly wasn't depressed.

The truth was, someone had cheated on me, I was lost in my career and had a lot of debts. I'm sure there have been so many who have been through a lot worse.

This isn't about how hard we've had it, as we've all been through something to varying degrees. It is about recognizing that there is more for us to experience no matter what has happened to us previously and no matter where we are at right now.

There is always room for us to grow and an infinite number of ways for our life to blossom beyond what we ever thought possible. We don't need to be going through some total meltdown or be experiencing severe emotional trauma, addiction, or depression to get value from this work, and I think therein lies the issue.

A lot will never discover the world of Self Love and Spirituality as they aren't searching for it. A lot won't commit to the inner work because they don't realise that they need it. They don't recognize themselves as needing support with their mindset or self-worth or confidence.

They don't realize that they can use The Laws of The Universe to create a life bigger and better than they ever imagined possible. I certainly didn't realize this work was something I really needed (and had perhaps needed for a while) until I started doing it. I thought that what I was experiencing was in the realm of what was normal and something I should just get on with. I felt that I was meant to just "suck it up" and "soldier on." But now, I see that we can all benefit from this work and reap the rewards that it can provide.

Let me first take you back to when I first discovered the world of mindset, Self Love, the Law of Attraction, and spirituality. I was in my mid-twenties and on paper. It would seem that I didn't really have much to complain about. I was in a good job working in London. I had a diamond ring on my finger, having recently got engaged. I had great friends and a loving family, and I had a shoe collection that would put Carrie Bradshaw to shame.

In theory, I should have been content. I had done what I "should" in that I'd studied hard, I'd got good grades, I'd gone to a great University, I'd took some time out to travel, I'd been to Law School, and I'd managed to land a job despite the fact we were coming out of the one of the worst recessions ever.

Some people may have looked at my life and would have thought that I had it all figured out; however, behind closed doors was a different story.

While on the surface I tried to make out like I had it all together, if anyone dug a little deeper, they would have discovered that I was, in fact, feeling utterly lost and deeply unfulfilled to the point that I'd wake up each day and cry by the bucketload. My confidence and self-worth were at an all-time low, I was struggling with anxiety, and on the whole, I just didn't feel like me.

What probably made everything worse was that I didn't tell anyone how I was really feeling. A part of me thought that what I was going through wasn't worth mentioning to anyone. I assumed that everyone had their own problems, that no one's life is perfect, and that there were plenty of people going through much worse than what I was.

Another part of me didn't want people to know that I was struggling. I'd always been the confident, outgoing, social butterfly, and I didn't want anyone to think any differently of me. Instead, I kept trying to brush things under the carpet and pretend that everything was fine. On the outside, I made it seem like I had it all together, yet underneath I was a mess.

There was one particular day where everything finally came to a head. This day started like many of my Monday's in London. It was raining (surprise, surprise) and "due to signal failure," my Tube was delayed. I'd hit the snooze button one too many times, so was already running late and, while legging it to the station like a madwoman, had managed to spill coffee down my dress. Just your average daily commute.

When my train finally showed up, I had to wrestle myself into a carriage in true survival of the fittest mode, taking out a man and his briefcase with my elbows to secure my place. By this point, I was sweating profusely in all my layers as, despite the bitterly cold London drizzle (ahh the delights of British Summer Time), inside the Tube, it was hotter than the sun. As some man in a suit wafted his Financial Times in my face for the fifth time that morning, huffing in frustration and getting redder by the second, I began to wonder exactly how I ended up feeling so disheartened as to how life was unfolding for me. I'd gone from being a fresh Uni grad with big dreams about becoming this high flying City Lawyer, to an overworked and underpaid employee who plodded along each day to a job that I knew deep down was not my life's calling.

It got to the point where the lack of fulfillment and direction in my career was causing me major anxiety to the point that most days, I'd leave for work crying and return home crying. I felt utterly lost and in desperate need of a change but had no idea of what to do as an alternative. I just assumed it was something I had to suck up and get on with. No one really enjoys their job anyway, *right*?!

Interestingly though, my real trigger for change wasn't my work, but my relationship. It wasn't a relationship I'd ever felt particularly secure in. There were a few suspicious messages that I'd turned a blind eye to, but deep down, things just didn't feel quite right. A woman's intuition is a powerful thing, and at the back of my mind, I knew there was something not entirely trustworthy about him. It had got to the point where I'd started checking his phone for evidence of betrayal and almost felt annoyed when I didn't find anything. I'd started to think that maybe I was going a bit bonkers.

I'd never been the jealous type, but I started conjuring up all of these scenarios in my head of what he was up to when my back was turned. The relationship was not bringing out the best in me. I was morphing into a person I didn't recognize, but at this point, I had no concrete evidence that he was actually doing anything wrong.

I remember one Saturday night, he just seemed to disappear while we were out with friends and then stumbled home the following morning without any sort of explanation. When I questioned him about where he was, he made me feel like I was being overly insecure and a nag. The current me would have told my younger self to leave immediately and to have trusted my gut, but by this point, I became convinced that I was the issue. I just needed to "be a better girlfriend," and all would be ok.

As it happened, my hunch turned out to be pretty accurate. As I made my way to my soul-destroying job on the Tube that fateful Monday morning, I felt my phone vibrate in my pocket. It was a message from a number I didn't recognize. Opening up the message and reading the words, I felt my heart drop. The message was from someone telling me that my dearly beloved hadn't entirely been acting as a fiancee should and that they thought it fair that I knew.

I remember feeling dizzy, sick, and my face started to burn. By the time the Tube finally arrived at my stop, my head was whirling a million miles per hour with all of these different thoughts and emotions.

Weirdly, I felt a little bit relieved when I started to digest what I'd just found out. I was relieved that I wasn't a crazy jealous psycho after all and that my hunch had been accurate. But after that came the self-loathing ("how could I have been so stupid not to have realized sooner!"), the shame ("how am I to tell everyone that the wedding is off!") and soon enough, my confidence came to a crushingly all-time low.

I don't remember much about the rest of the day, nor do I remember much about how I came home that evening and ended things. It all feels a bit of a blur now, and I think I was in such a state of shock, sadness, anger, and overwhelm that I've blocked a lot of what happened out of memory.

I remember saying the words "I deserve better," but at the time, not entirely believing it. A part of me felt like things were my fault. It's funny how somebody can do something to you that is entirely out of your control, yet you still think you are partly to blame. I started to think that maybe, because I'd been so miserable in my work, perhaps he was just fed up with my complaining. I was angry at him, but equally, I was angry at myself.

The cherry on the cake was the fact that during the time we'd been together, I'd been soothing my pain in the form of shopping. Shopping was my form of escape from having to think about how unhappy I felt in my career or how insecure I felt in my relationship, and I'd been hitting up the online stores like a woman possessed, accumulating over £20k worth of credit card debt.

For anyone who has ever suffered with debt will understand, it places a huge emotional weight over you. I felt suffocated by it, and I struggled to figure out how I would ever be able to pay it off. Looking back now, I don't really know what exactly I spent all of the money on. I certainly don't have any significant purchases that spring to mind.

Spending and shopping was my emotional release, a short term thrill which helped me feel better for a short while and block out the realities of life that were bringing me down. Some people choose to numb themselves with alcohol or drugs or sex. My drugs of choice were called "Topshop" and "Zara."

Thankfully, one of the things that I have drastically been able to change since embarking on my spiritual journey has been my finances. In fact, my business now regularly makes more in one month than what I would previously make in a whole year in my job. While some of this change can be accredited to things I've done and action steps I've taken, I know that a big part of my rapid change to my financial circumstances has been my mindset.

A huge part of our money story relates to our sense of worth and how we love and respect ourselves. When we make poor financial choices or experience a lot of negative circumstances relating to money, it's often because of deeply ingrained limiting beliefs about ourselves. I will go into this in more detail in this book because I know that a lot of people reading this won't be where they want to be financially and what I want to share with you has the power to transform your bank account for the better.

So, there I found myself, with one failed engagement under my belt, feeling incredibly lost in terms of my job and with a boatload of debt, but it was from this place that I started to dip my toe into the world of mindset and spirituality. The week after I found out about the cheating fiancee, I found myself lurking in the self-help aisle of my local bookshop looking for some sort of answer to jump out at me, and it was *"The Power of Now "* by Eckhart Tolle that caught my eye.

I was desperate for something, anything that would make me feel better, and as someone who'd always found comfort in the pages of books, I believed in the power of words to heal. My daily commute went from being one of the worst parts of my day to my safe haven. Absorbing the words on the pages, I would block out the noise as I felt myself shift from heart-wrenching emotional pain and sadness to a feeling of hope.

Slowly, I began to be able to detach myself from the negative thought patterns, swatting them away like pesky flies. I was able to experience a stillness in my mind, a place where there was no anxiety, fear, worries, or sorrow. This emptiness made me feel emotions I'd never felt in a long time - excitement, enthusiasm, optimism.

Although I didn't realize it at the time, this feeling was my vibration rising. I was in the high vibe space I needed to be in to co-create with The Universe, a magical, tingling electric place where, if I just directed my thoughts in the right way, I could be, do and have anything my heart desired.

The issue was, at this point, I still had a total lack of clarity when it came to my thoughts. I didn't know what I wanted or who I wanted to be. While I was able to get myself to a place of feeling amazing through meditation and mindfulness, there was still a lot of work to do before I was able to manifest a life that set my soul on fire.

I knew I needed to dive deeper, which is what led me to the Law of Attraction. I'd read The Secret years earlier, so it was this book that I turned to first, and while it certainly helped me understand more about the power of my thoughts to create my reality, It still left me with a lot of questions. Over the next few months, I began to devour anything I could get my hands on — books on spirituality, self-worth, mindset, Law of Attraction, The Divine Feminine. I was hungry for whatever would make me feel better.

I fully immersed myself in this world, nurturing my heart and soul, spending the time for myself and my own healing. Slowly but surely, I started to feel "ready." Ready for what, I wasn't quite sure at this point, but I knew something BIG was coming. I felt bold and empowered and, armed with a newfound confidence, I felt ready to start my next chapter.

Of course, I still had no idea what that next chapter looked like. I still had zero clue as to what to do for a career. I still had so many lessons to learn about myself and who I wanted to be and the impact I wanted to have on the world, but something had lit a fire inside of me. Something was telling me that how my story had started didn't need to be how it ended, and right now, I had the power to create my life how I wanted it.

Fast forward a few months later, and I'd not only left my fiancée and all thoughts of him behind me, but I'd also quit my job and booked myself on a flight to Switzerland to work as a chalet girl. I'd swapped city life for cleaning and cooking for demanding guests in the high-end Ski resort of Verbier. Did I have a plan? Not really. But what I did know was that from now on, I'd be doing things my way, for me.

Switzerland turned out to be incredible, possibly the best five months of my life. I skied every day, met friends that I know I will have for life and, the cherry on the cake, was that I also met

Philip, the guy who I now know I will spend the rest of my life with and who has since become the father to my daughter, Raffi.

Did I "find myself" at the top of a mountain? Not quite. But I knew that taking that leap into the unknown was the start of a new me, a me who wasn't afraid of taking chances, a me who followed her heart and desires, a me who was starting to embrace who I really was and make choices based on what really lit me up.

Now sadly, a ski season isn't forever, so ultimately, I knew I had to return home and face reality, but I was doing so feeling optimistic about my future. Returning to London once the snow melted, I made a commitment to myself to continue with my spiritual path, to commit to the inner work, and explore where it would take me. It was on this journey that I discovered the coaching industry.

Coaching, as it turned out, was the thing I felt like I'd been searching for most of my life. When I enrolled in my first coaching program, it was like a light had all of a sudden been switched on. Not only did coaching allow me to go deeper into the work I'd already been doing on myself, but it also opened up for me an avenue to explore my own purpose in this world.

As I began to understand myself with much more clarity, I realized that the rollercoaster of the past few years could be turned into my career. The passion I had for personal growth and spirituality could become my purpose. My wounds could be turned to wisdom, and I could become someone who lit the path for other women who needed support and guidance after finding themselves lost, unfulfilled, or struggling with their self-worth.

The coaching industry spoke my language, and it didn't take me long to decide that this was a career path I wanted to pursue. It was a world that would allow me to make the impact I knew I was destined to make while also being able to transform my own life in the process.

Fast forward to the present day, and I have a business that has become far bigger than I ever imagined. My company, The Clique, is a company that has to date served thousands of women across the globe, helping them step into their power and rise up as the confident women they are destined to be. The Clique has also helped hundreds of those women create their own success stories as a coach through our coaching certification program, The Clique Academy. Many of those women have since gone on to create their own six-figure global coaching empires through our business and mindset course, The Clique Elite.

Seeing the women we work with making these incredible changes in their life has been my biggest source of joy over the past few years. There is nothing more rewarding than witnessing brilliant women get out of their own way and go for what they want unapologetically. This is what I want for you too.

What I will share in the chapters that follow is a process that has been the catalyst for my own growth and the growth of many of my clients. It is a framework that weaves together all of the tools, rituals, and strategies that have helped me become the woman I needed to be to get me to where I want to go and create unstoppable success, abundance, and fulfillment in my life. It's a process that I am hugely passionate about sharing with as many people as possible as I knew that once you become armed with this know-how, you can be, do and have anything your heart desires. Not only will this process help you feel incredible and uplifted and empowered, but it will help you to start witnessing the magic of manifesting with The Universe. Whatever you can see in your mind can and should be yours when you implement this process into your life.

I named the process Self Love & Spiritual Alchemy because it is designed to not only help you strengthen your self-worth and cultivate true Self Love, but will also help you to expand your spiritual gifts and get the Law of Attraction to work in your favor.

Manifesting is a pretty magical process when you understand how to attract your desires. Once you begin to witness incredible things, people, opportunities, success, and money come into your life, you will discover that we live in an infinite Universe where settling needn't be our default way of living. I no longer settle in my life for less than what I know I deserve, neither do my clients, and neither should you.

What I hope to inspire you to realize through the pages of this book is that you have a power far greater than you know. While this book encourages you to transform your inner world, this is not about becoming someone else or trying to be something you are not. This work is about tapping into the gifts that are already buried within you, gifts that you perhaps haven't even realized you possess.

You are more capable than what you give yourself credit for, and it's time for your authentic light to shine in the brightest way possible.

Don't hide your magic.

The world needs you to step up, rise up, and become the powerful goddess you are meant to be. Now is your time to become the woman who doesn't put her dreams on hold, doesn't let fear hold her back, believes in her abilities and trusts that The Universe is divinely guiding her every step of the way.

I've got you, I'm here for you, and I cannot wait for you to witness the wonders that Self Love & Spiritual Alchemy can ignite for you. Now let's do this.

The Twelve Universal Laws

What you think, you become. What you feel, you attract. What you imagine, you create ~Buddha

If you are ready to start creating a life by design rather than by default, then you are in the right place.

Self Love & Spiritual Alchemy is a framework for how to transform your inner world so that you can manifest the life that you truly desire and rise up as the confident and empowered goddess you were born to be.

The process detailed in this book is based upon my Self Love & Spiritual Alchemy coaching program. This program is a twelve-week, deeply transformational, mindset experience where I work with my clients to guide them through the inner shifts they need to make to manifest the life of their dreams.

Underpinning this framework are the twelve Universal Laws of The Universe. These twelve Universal Laws, when working in your favour, can help you transform your reality into something bigger and better than you ever dreamed possible. To start with, I'd like to introduce you to these laws, and I'll start with the law that many of you will have already heard of:

The Law of Attraction.

This is the law that states that like attracts like and your thoughts, beliefs, and energy create your outer world. Maybe you've heard of the Law of Attraction, or perhaps this is new territory for you. Either way, my guess is that you have probably manifested some things into your life that you didn't really want.

Maybe it's a bad relationship, a lack of a relationship, financial trouble, sickness, or just a general feeling of unfulfillment. Whatever you've got going on in your life right now that doesn't reflect who you really want to be, how you really want to live and how you really want to feel, the process I will guide you through inside the pages of this book will help you change all of that.

Some of you reading this may have tried to put the Law of Attraction into practice but haven't seen the kind of results you were hoping for and perhaps are currently doubtful about whether it actually works. Let me just start by saying that the Law of Attraction works, and it doesn't just work some of the time and for some people, it works all of the time and for everyone. It's a law, just like the Law of Gravity is a law and is always working, so is the Law of Attraction.

If you are experiencing something in your life right now that you'd rather not, it's not that the law isn't working, it's simply that you haven't figured out how to get the Law of Attraction to work in your favour.

Self Love & Spiritual Alchemy is designed to help you with this, and I will start by sharing that the biggest reason why people don't see success with The Law of Attraction is that they don't take into consideration the other laws of The Universe. While The Law of Attraction got a lot of press from books such as The Secret, which sold millions of copies worldwide, most people don't actually realise that there are in fact twelve Universal Laws in total.

Used in isolation, it may be difficult to get the kinds of results you want from the Law of Attraction which is why it's important to appreciate what these other laws are. Let's start by going through these laws in more detail.

The Law of Inspired Action

We will start with The Law of Inspired Action. One of the biggest misconceptions about the Law of Attraction is that it just takes a bit of positive thinking for positive things to drop into your lap.

As lovely as it would be for a Gucci handbag or Ryan Gosling to just fall out of the sky and into your possession, things don't quite work like that. There has to be some kind of action on your part to put the wheels in motion.

You are co-creating with The Universe, meaning you can't just think about what you want and The Universe will send it to you. You have to show up and play your part too. This is where the Law of Inspired Action comes into play.

You have to take inspired action towards creating the life that you want, with an emphasis on the "inspired" part. The action you take has to feel good. It has to be action that feels joyful and light and easy. It has to feel fun and uplifting. It has to feel authentic to you and be true to what really lights you up. If you take action that causes you to feel stressed, that makes you feel shitty about yourself, or that feels inauthentic to you, that's not going to cut it.

If you take action that feels forced, that's also not going to cut it. Inspired action is about choosing to do the things that keep you in alignment as much as possible, action that helps you feel good and helps you maintain a high vibration. This leads me onto the next law which is The Law of Vibration.

The Law of Vibration.

The Law of Vibration dictates that everything on this planet is in a constant state of movement. When we look at our hand, while we may see it as a solid object, the reality is that our hand is made up of millions of tiny particles of energy that are constantly moving, or rather, vibrating.

The same is true for everything on this planet. Everything has its own specific energetic frequency with some things vibrating quickly and at a high vibration, with other things vibrating slowly and at a low frequency.

Now if we tie this in with the Law of Attraction, like attracts like, meaning that high vibrational things are a magnet to other high vibrational things. If you are vibrating at a high frequency, you will attract more high vibe things into your life.

It's not enough to just talk about what you want then it appears in your life. You can talk about all of the amazing things you want in your life and create a vision board with all of your dreams on it, but if internally you are vibrating at a low frequency because of fears, doubts or low self-worth, you will struggle to manifest your desires into your life.

This is why a lot of people who create a vision board don't get it to work for them. They tell The Universe what they want but don't then work on raising their vibration so that they become a vibrational match to what they want to attract.

The Law of Divine Oneness.

This is the law that says everything in our world is interconnected. Everything you do, say, believe, and desire will have an impact on the world and those around you. In the same way, what others do, say, desire and believe will also have an impact on your life.

The impact may sometimes happen straight away and be easy to spot, but this isn't always the case. It can sometimes take a while for the change to manifest, and the change may be a subtle one.

When it comes to getting what you want in life, you need to remember this law and remember that we don't exist in a vacuum. Our personal experiences can be shaped by what others say, do, believe and desire.

This law has particular importance when it comes to our beliefs. Our beliefs shape our reality. What we believe about ourselves and the world around us has an impact on what we then experience in our lives. Often, the beliefs we possess are not just ours, but the beliefs of those who surround us. This is The Law of Divine Oneness at work.

These beliefs that we absorb from others can change the way we think and act and shape our lives for better or for worse. I've become obsessed with belief work and reprogramming my own beliefs and the beliefs of my clients so that they match the reality that they want to create.

For example, some of my clients join my coaching program as they want to transform their finances and create more wealth in their lives. To do this, we need to examine what their current beliefs are around money and where they possess limiting beliefs about money that are creating a negative money experience in their life.

So, for example, if you believe that making money is hard work, you will create a life where making money is hard work. You may find yourself in a job where you are working incredibly long hours to earn the money you desire.

These beliefs have often been passed into use by those who have raised us. So maybe you had a father who worked incredibly hard for his money. His belief may have then been subsequently passed onto you, and you then create the same kind of reality, finding yourself continually pushing and hustling to bring money into your life. It's therefore essential to examine our beliefs and how they may have been shaped by the people in our lives, specifically those beliefs which are negatively impacting our existence.

The Law of Correspondence

The Law of Correspondence dictates that your outer world reflects your inner world. Whatever is going on externally is a mirror of what is happening internally. If there is something we are not happy about within ourselves, this will be displayed in the outer world.

When you have a negative experience, this is caused by some disharmony in your inner world. This is why how we feel about ourselves is so important. If on the inside you are unkind to yourself, feeling bad about yourself, telling yourself

"I'm no good at that" or "I'm too fat/too thin/too old," or whatever your thought process is, this causes you to feel negative emotions.

That feeling then creates negative experiences in your reality. The Law of Perpetual Transmutation of Energy This law dictates that everything around us is in a constant state of change. Many of these changes aren't visible to the human eye because they are at a cellular level.

This law is important because, with this law, you can trigger positive changes in your vibration. So, if you are vibrating at a low frequency and feeling sad, angry or frustrated, if you surround yourself with high vibe people, people who are happy, optimistic and joyful, this will trigger energy transmutation in you.

Your energy will change to a high vibration, and you will feel yourself also becoming happy, optimistic and joyful. With this law, we needn't accept that how things are will always need to be the case.

If we are sad now, we can surround ourselves with positive energy, whether it is positive people or environments or positive things. Their energy can transmute ours and help us feel better. We have the power to change our vibration and with that change, manifest amazing experiences and things into our world.

The Law of Cause & Effect

This law dictates that all action has a corresponding reaction, meaning that your life can impact the world around you and cause either a positive or negative reaction. Similarly, your physical surroundings can impact your life.

Think about how you feel when you are somewhere you really love, perhaps at the spa or on a beautiful beach. What kind of effect does this have on you? Maybe you feel relaxed or happy? This is the Law of Cause and Effect at work. Your environment is causing you to have a certain physical reaction.

The Law of Compensation

The Law of Compensation dictates that you will get back what you give. Think about this law as Karma. You get out of the world what you are willing to put into it. You reap what you sow.

If you are a shitty person who always spreads hate, you can expect to receive the same kind of negativity boomerang back to you. While I'm sure that anyone reading this book wouldn't intentionally want to cause harm or upset to others, often, through our own feelings of inadequacy and low self-worth, we project our negative emotions onto others. This may take the form of anger, frustration, jealousy or distrust.

Whichever of these negative feelings you give out, The Law of Compensation results in similar negativity bouncing back to us.

The Law of Relativity

This law dictates that everything is neutral until it is compared to something else. So, for example, someone cannot be classed as either rich nor poor until we've measured them against someone else's wealth. We need to be able to make a comparison before we can make an assessment on something. What we compare something to is going to dictate how we evaluate something.

So let's say you are in a room full of billionaires, chances are you will feel poor in comparison. But if you put yourself in a room full of people who are unemployed, chances are you may feel wealthy in comparison.

Everything is relative. This law has relevance to manifesting our desires because it can help us get to a place of gratitude. If we compare ourselves to those who are a lot less fortunate than we are, we can feel incredibly lucky, successful, wealthy. We feel thankful for what we have and allow ourselves to appreciate all the good in our lives.

Equally, however, this law can push our desires further away. When we constantly compare ourselves to others who have already achieved so much more than what we have or have created so much more amounts of success and wealth, it can leave us feeling that what we have isn't enough.

The Law of Polarity

This law states that everything has an opposite, and these opposites allow us to understand our life. It's opposites that also help us to get clear on what we want. We can get clarity on what we want though experiencing what we don't want. Without pain, there can't be Love. Opposites are therefore necessary for us to experience our desires. Discovering more of what we don't want leads us closer to what we do want.

For example, I spent a number of years working in the corporate world. This wasn't a pleasant experience for me, but it did help me to get more clarity on what I wanted. Through my work, I had identified lots of things I didn't like: a lack of freedom, working for a boss, being tied to a desk all day, having to work very rigid hours. In experiencing these things, my vision of what I did want from my career became a lot clearer. Perhaps my business wouldn't exist today if I hadn't been able to have that contrast.

The Law of Perpetual Motion

The Law of Perpetual Motion is all about cycles. Cycles exist across nature. Think about your womanly cycles, the moon cycles or the circle of life itself. Everything in nature is cyclic. It's important to recognise the role these cycles play in relation to our desires and creating the life we want. I've become obsessed with tuning into these cycles because I've found that going with nature rather than against it, I've been able to create my life in a way that feels good.

So often we live our lives in a very linear way, trying to get from A to B without honouring our own rhythms or the rhythms of nature. Think about a time when you may have tried to work to a deadline, and it left you feeling burned out and exhausted. You continue to work despite nature telling you to slow down. Going against natures' cycles leads us to feel like we are pushing against things or trying to force things rather than allowing things to happen as they should.

The law of gender

The law of gender is all about feminine and masculine energies. Masculine Energy is action-orientated. It's about getting things done. This type of energy is competitive, power-hungry.

On the other hand, Feminine Energy is much more about allowing and receiving. It's collaborative, and it's nurturing. We all have both types of energy present within us, but there must be the right balance of these energies for us to live authentic and happy lives.

Unfortunately, we live in a society where Masculine Energy has become the dominant force. Think about how most big businesses are run. It's all about beating the competition, being the best, hustling hard. Because we have been subjected to this so much that we believe it to be the norm, a lot of women live sitting far too much into their masculine energy, and this can actually hold them back further from living the life they want or feeling how they want to feel.

So where does Self Love come into all of this?

Well, from my experience, we cannot manifest our desires when we are coming from a place of hating ourselves, talking negatively about ourselves or just generally not treating ourselves with the love and respect we deserve.

The Laws of The Universe, Self Love & achieving our desires are all intertwined. Remember; like attracts like, so if we want to attract love, abundance, success, amazing relationships and excellent health into our lives, it all starts with recognising we are worthy of those things. We have to love, honour and respect ourselves before we can attract incredible experiences, people and things. When we are plagued with self-loathing, fears, limiting beliefs, self-doubt, and low confidence, we hold ourselves apart from receiving the amazing gifts from The Universe.

How you think and feel about yourself sets the tone for what you attract and experience in your reality. It may be a hard pill to swallow because it requires us to face up to the fact that we have created our current circumstances; however, with this knowledge comes the power to change.

If we can create a life that we don't want, we can equally and just as easily create a life that we do want. Once we learn to truly love ourselves, we become a magnet to more amazing people, things and experiences.

Self Love isn't just about self-care. While self-care is an essential part of Self Love, true Self Love is not just a thing that makes you feel good for a little while. True Self Love is a lasting transformation from within. When you commit to true Self Love, your whole world can transform for the better, and you start to witness the most incredible things in your life.

Whether it's in your finances, your career, your health, or your relationships, manifesting amazing things happens when we believe we are worthy and deserving of anything we desire. Manifesting amazing things happens when we are kind to ourselves and love ourselves, not when we are talking down to ourselves.

Remember: your inner world creates your outer world. If you are holding onto deep-rooted beliefs about not being good enough, about failure, about not being loveable, about not being worthy or deserving of success, about not being smart enough, or about not being pretty enough, no amount of Charlotte Tilbury makeup or trips to the hairdressers is going to change that. Self Love, therefore, has to be made a priority.

Now maybe you're reading this right now, and at the back of your mind, you are thinking that all of this talk of Universal Laws and thoughts becoming things sounds a little bit "woo woo" for your liking and I get it. The old me would have probably scoffed at some of the things I'm going to share with you, but I urge you to keep an open mind. If you do what you've always done, you will get what you've always got and sometimes, we need to try different things, enter new territories and open our mind up to new ways of thinking if we are going to expand our life in new directions.

My mission is not to convince you that the Law of Attraction works, but one thing you can do to strengthen your faith that The Universe is listening and conspiring to give you exactly want is to conduct the exercise at the end of the chapter and spend the next 24 hours completely open to the idea that The Universe is going to deliver you some sort of gift.

You have to expect that miracles are waiting for you if you want to experience them and you have to be in happy anticipation that what you want could appear at any given moment.

Exercise - Strengthen Your Faith in The Universe

If you are new to this world and want a little reassurance that The Universe is working in your favour, I'd like to invite you to spend the next 24 hours completely open to the idea that The Universe is going to deliver you some sort of gift.

Specify what that gift is, something that right now, you could believe could be delivered to you. You will soon learn the importance of beliefs, and we can only attract something if we genuinely believe it is possible, so don't choose "a lottery win" or "manifesting £1million pound".

Pick something that you have some belief around it being possible.
So it may be that you invite The Universe to send you a white feather or a specific make of car or a pink flamingo.

Choose something that you don't necessarily see all the time. Then, once you've set your intention about what you want to receive, spend the next 24 hours expecting to see it.

Search for it. Keep your eyes open to seeing it.

Make a note of your findings and for each time you see your gift from The Universe, remind yourself that when you ask, The Universe always delivers.

Clarity

Clarity is the most important thing. If you are not clear, nothing is going to happen ~ Diane Von Furstenberg

A number of years ago, a few of my friends and I went to Ibiza for a Rosé fuelled long weekend. I love Ibiza as it caters to my love of dancing, great food and sunsets with a bit of yoga thrown into the mix. There is something quite electric about the island, which is perhaps why I had one of my first major "a-ha" moments while I was there.

Yes, it's very much a "party island", but for me, Ibiza is so much more than just a place to dance until sunrise. The laid back, boho vibe speaks to my soul, and it's a place where one day, I imagine hosting deeply transformational retreats and spiritual gatherings for groups of like-minded women from my hilltop Finca.

Anyway, my "a-ha" moment was triggered in the same way I'm sure many others before me have experienced life-changing realisations in that I was about five hours into a daytime drinking session with my friends.

I'm sure I'm not the only woman who has had a major life breakthrough while under the influence of wine, and I'm sure I won't be the last, but as I learnt a lesson that day that has stuck with me and is a lesson I've since passed onto hundreds of my clients.

On day one of our trip, my friends and I had decided to head to one of Ibiza's many beach clubs and had in our possession these giant, pink, inflatable swans. After we were one or two bottles of Rosé down, we decided it would be a brilliant idea to take our inflatable swans into the sea for a little dip. With drinks in one hand and inflatables hooked under an arm, off we went.

After about thirty minutes or so of bobbing along on the waves, sun on our faces and not a care in the world, it suddenly dawned on us that we had drifted pretty far from the shore. Now, I'm certainly no Olympic swimmer, but I wasn't too worried at this point. We weren't that far away from the beach, and I was sure that with a bit of oomph, we'd be back to safety in no time. Launching ourselves off our swans, we started to kick. Only, the tide was against us, and we soon realised that we were kicking and kicking but not moving anywhere fast.

Ten minutes of kicking later, we realised that we were now even further away from when we started. By this point, the panic started to kick in, and we started to yell at the revellers on the beach for help. Of course, with the Balearic beats pumping away, no one took the slightest bit of notice.

It was the hottest part of the day, and my face was beginning to sting from the sun. Our fate didn't look good. I had visions of us drifting all the way to Africa, arriving on another continent burnt to a crisp. Thankfully, things didn't escalate quite that far. We had been spotted by a boat making its way to our beach club, filled with German party goers. We were saved, although our dignities were left in pieces, as we sped back to safety.

Now you might be thinking "I picked up this book thinking I was going to get guidance on Self Love & Spiritual enlightenment, not to hear tales of drunk English girls nearly drowning on their inflatable swans." Keep with me; the story does have a point (I promise!)

When we got back to the beach, we thought it best to keep our heads down and keep things low key for the rest of the day. We'd already had far too much excitement, sun and alcohol for one afternoon. Sprawling myself onto my sun lounger, I took some time to recover from our near-death experience. Now it may seem a tad dramatic, but I started to think about what if we had floated all the way to Africa? What if the boat hadn't spotted us? What if we hadn't made it back?

I then started to think about all of the things in my life that I hadn't had a chance to do; Find a career I was passionate about, travel more, have children, write a book, become best friends with Oprah...

My mind whirled a million miles per hour as I contemplated "life" and I suddenly thought that our little escapade on the swans carried an important lesson. We had mounted our swans without any real thought about where we were heading. We hadn't set any goal about which direction to go in. We had coasted along without any real intention, and soon enough, we ended up somewhere we really didn't want to be and finding it incredibly difficult to pull ourselves back.

It dawned on me that this is how so many people live their lives, myself included. We bob along, without much thought about where we are going, or whether where we are heading is somewhere we really intend to get to and soon enough, we find ourselves lost, stuck, and swimming against the tide.

I had spent the majority of my twenties like this. Sure, I had some vague notion of where I wanted to go. I knew I wanted to be successful, to have a good career, to be financially stable, to have a great relationship, but I had never been very specific about the details. I hadn't been very intentional about whether where I was heading was somewhere I really wanted to go and then found myself in a position I really didn't want to be in.

I was in a career that left me unfulfilled, a relationship that was shattering my confidence and I had gotten myself so far into debt I had no idea how I was ever going to get myself out of it. I hadn't chosen any of these things. I had coasted into them. I had been unintentional about what I really wanted, therefore it's no surprise that I got something far removed from what I really desired deep down.

And this brings me to the first part of true Self Love and manifesting the life of your wildest dreams; You have to give yourself the time and space you need to get clear on exactly what you want. You owe this to yourself. And I don't just mean "shower thinking". Pondering over your desires for a few minutes every now and then whilst you get ready for your day isn't going to cut it. I mean sitting down and carving out a specific amount of time to get really intentional about exactly what it is you want from life.

Who do you want to be? How do you want to feel? What is the impact you want to make on the world? Who are the people that you want to surround yourself with? What kind of money do you want to see in your bank account? You have to let The Universe know all of the little nitty-gritty details. Most people don't give themselves this luxury.

True Self Love means carving out time in your busy schedule to make this work a non-negotiable and letting The Universe know exactly what your heart desires. The more specific you can get with this, the better.

Imagine you gave your partner a request to go out shopping and buy you a dress. Now, maybe your partner is Gok Wan and knows exactly what dress you need but, chances are, your partner comes back with a dress in the wrong size, wrong colour and totally wrong style. Yes, you received a dress, but it's completely far removed from what you were really asking for. Because you didn't get clear on what you wanted, you failed to receive what you really wanted. The same is true for anything we want in life. Unless you let The Universe know the details of your desires, don't be surprised if you end up with something that looks completely different to what you were asking for.

The issue with our desires, however, is that many of us simply don't know what we really want. I truly believe that this is because we are so used to being led by what is expected of us from others or by society, that we aren't used to asking ourselves whether our choices match up with our true desires.

For many of us, parents, teachers and society influence our thoughts so much that we end up making choices based on what we think we should do, rather than what actually lights us up. For many of us, we don't allow ourselves enough time or space to think beyond what we have been told, shown or led to believe. I think the following quote sums this up perfectly.

"If you don't get out of the box you've been raised in, you won't understand how much bigger the world is."
~ Angelina Jolie

I started a career in Law not because it was my burning passion, but because I didn't really know what else to do as an alternative. Society had told me it was a "good job" that paid well. I had parents and teachers telling me what a fantastic choice it would be. I spoke with other lawyers who had been climbing the career ladder who spoke of their successes. Rather than being completely true to my own passions, values and desires, I just went along with what was expected of me. When I realised that actually, I hated corporate life, I assumed that I'd have to just get on with it and that no one really likes their job anyway.

For years, I denied myself the luxury of even considering other options. I buried my passion for writing and being creative, I ignored my calling to inspire, and I stifled my entrepreneurial spirit. I figured that I'd sealed my fate and I should just get on with my legal career, even if it wasn't really rocking my world.

Now, I can see that this was a huge mistake, a mistake that I don't think I'm alone in making. I had suppressed my true desires to follow along with the status quo. I had ignored what really brought me joy because I believed pursuing those things wasn't really possible for me.

While the idea of running my own business had always been appealing, I'd never really considered entrepreneurship because deep down, I didn't really think it was possible for me to be hugely successful in business. I assumed that I'd need huge amounts of money to start (money that I didn't have). I assumed I'd need to have some incredible business idea or life-changing product. I assumed that I'd need to struggle for years and years to make it. All of these limiting beliefs had held me back from taking action, and as a result, I coasted along in jobs that didn't fulfil me.

Within this book, I will be diving into how to ditch these limiting beliefs, but for now, I want to help you connect to some of your desires. To get things started, I want to help you get intentional about where you want to go in life, a process that begins with getting intentional about how you start your day.

I'm a huge advocate of waking up with intention and clarity, not just about what you want to achieve that day, but how you want your life to unfold moving forwards. I firmly believe that how we start our day sets the foundations for how we ultimately live our lives.

What I'm about to reveal to you is the greatest gift you can give to yourself. Forget the Gucci handbag; this gift costs you nothing and will make you feel like a million dollars every single day. The gift I am talking about is the gift of a purposeful morning routine, and I want to share with you the morning ritual that has propelled my life in forwards in the most amazing ways.

For many people, the thought of having a leisurely morning with time carved out for you and your own personal and spiritual development is a bit of a luxury, but waking up each day with intention is one of the most powerful things you can do for yourself. My morning ritual has been one of the major changes I've made to my life that has completely transformed the way I feel, my energy, and what I'm able to manifest into my life.

I like to call it my Daily Goddess Ritual, as it makes me feel like a Goddess every single day - empowered, confident, and ready to take on the world.

Before I dive into my Daily Goddess Ritual in more detail, I'd like to take it back to my pre daily ritual days because I'm sure some of you reading this now will resonate with this. It used to be the case that my phone was the first thing that would command my attention. After hitting the snooze button multiple times, I'd hazily drag myself up and reach for my phone to scroll aimlessly through Instagram and Facebook.

This is another classic case of unintentional living. I had unintentionally created a habit of social media screen time every morning, a habit that wasn't serving me and instead, was leaving me feeling pretty shit about myself and the way my life was panning out. While the Instagram famous bloggers were showcasing their jet-set lifestyles, I was about to embark on an hour-long commute to a job that was making me feel more and more dissatisfied with life.

Rather than being inspired and motivated by what I was being shown on my news feed, it was leaving me feeling even more unfulfilled and deflated. How was it that some people managed to carve out these exciting, fun, creative careers and get paid to basically have a good time while I was struggling to make ends meet and working crazy hours in a career that I knew wasn't my calling?

After about fifteen minutes or so of looking longingly at my phone, my normal ritual was to then fly into a mad panic as I realised that I was going to be late for work. I'd charge around my room getting ready, rummaging into my chaotic underwear drawer trying to find a pair of matching socks, but failing, and ending up wearing one plain black trainer sock and another bright red festive number with reindeers patterned over it.

With zero time for breakfast, I'd throw myself out of the door and normally have to run to make it to the Tube. If there was one word to describe my morning it was "stressful" No matter what time I got up, I would always end up leaving late and generally feeling a little bit disgruntled with life.

It wasn't until I read a book by Hal Elrod called *"The Miracle Morning"* that everything transformed. It's a book that I urge everyone to read as for me, it was a game-changer. The book opened my eyes to the importance of a morning routine, and it got me thinking that how I was starting my day was setting the tone for how the rest of my day was going to pan out.

Let me just ask you something; Have you ever got up on the wrong side of the bed? You wake up late, you stump your toe, you spill your coffee down you, you miss your train. The day goes from bad to worse. A bad start to your day is a catalyst for more unwanted things to come into your life. This is the Law of Attraction at work

The Law of Attraction dictates that we like attracts like. If we start the day off on the wrong foot and it leaves us feeling pretty crappy, chances are we will invite more crappy experiences into our life for the rest of the day. But if you start the day in a way that leaves you feeling inspired and empowered, you are opening yourself up to wonderful opportunities, people and successes coming your way.

This is where a purposeful morning routine comes into play. Not only does it help you to start your day feeling incredible, but it also helps you to keep moving in the direction you really want.

If the Inflatable Swan story has taught us anything, it is that being unintentional about what we are doing or where we are going is dangerous. When we start our day without intention - hitting the snooze button on life and carrying on without any real regard for whether what we are doing or where we are heading is aligned with our souls purpose, who we really want to be or what we want to do - the next thing we realise is that ten years have passed and we find ourselves in a life that doesn't really set our soul on fire. It may be a "comfortable" life, but if we are totally honest with ourselves, deep down, we are left wanting more.

I myself had got to a point where I knew deep down I wanted more, but I wasn't sure what that "something more" really looked like. This morning ritual gave me the clarity I needed. It gave me time each day to really tune into my desires, my passions, my values and identify what really lit me up. It gave me the space I needed to explore what was available for me in a world where I could be, do and have anything. It allowed me to start thinking beyond any sorts of limitations I was putting on myself.

The morning ritual therefore serves two purposes; Firstly, it makes you feel amazing so that you attract more amazing things into your life. Secondly, it helps you get clear and intentional about your goals and what you really want and ensures you keep moving in a forward momentum towards that destination without drifting too far off course.

Let me start by going through what my Daily Goddess ritual consists of before I go into some of the steps in more detail. The ritual involves (in no particular order) meditation, reading or listening to something inspiring, journaling, affirmations, vision boarding, exercise, a cold shower and a celery juice.

How long you spend on each of these doesn't really matter. If you can only commit 10 minutes each morning, fine. If you can commit an hour, great. The important thing is that you commit to the ritual each day and if you do, I pinky promise that you will feel amazing. Now let's look into a few of the steps in more detail.

I'm going to start with visualisation because the purpose of this section is clarity and I want to reiterate the importance of getting clarity on exactly what you want in life and how to let The Universe know the specifics of your desires. Introducing Vision Boards.

The humble Vision Board is far more than just a fun thing to make and a chance to tune into our inner child by getting crafty. The Vision Board can be the springboard into a life bigger and better than your wildest dreams. Maybe you've made a Vision Board before and it didn't really work for you, or maybe you've heard about them but just see them as a bit of fun and not really something to live your life by. I'd had Vision Boards myself in the past, but I don't think I'd ever really used them as I should. It wasn't until I started to do the inner work that I really started to take them seriously as a tool that could help me step into the life I knew I was meant for.

My first real experience of my Vision Board working was back when my partner, Philip, and I were co-sharing a flat in London. We were pretty broke at the time. I was trying to pay off my years and years of credit card debt and Philip was getting paid £3.50 an hour as an electrical apprentice.

We had fallen in love with a leafy area of London, Fulham, which also happened to be way out of our price bracket in terms of rent. Rather than finding a cheaper area to live in, we ended up living in the living room of a two-bedroom flat we shared with far too many flatmates.

It wasn't ideal on so many levels, but it was all that we could afford and, having started on my personal and spiritual development journey, I knew that I was moving onto bigger and better things. My current situation was not an indication of my future. I knew I was in the process of creating a life of abundance, a life where I didn't have to shack up with some bloke we found on Gumtree that only showered every few weeks.

My Vision Boards mapped out my future, a future that was exciting, luxurious, high vibe and inspiring. I say Vision Boards (plural) because I like to map things out based on short, medium and long term goals and like to make separate boards accordingly.

Property has always been one of the key features of my vision boards. My "Ultimate Vision Board" is a combination of beautiful Georgian mansions, hilltop Finca's with infinity pools overlooking the Balearic seas and snow-topped Chalet's in a chic ski resort, complete with the obligatory hot tub on the terrace overlooking the mountain view.

My short term vision board was a little more humble in terms of property goals. A small flat that we could call our own rather than needing to share, complete with a spare room which would become my office. At this point, I was working from my laptop while sitting in bed as I had no other options. I couldn't wait to have a space that I could call my own.

At the time, I was very much into the Scandinavian, minimalist "clean" look, so the flat on my vision board was all light and airy colours. The walls were bright white, and the floors were pale grey carpets. My favourite room I'd pinned though was the bathroom - a grey and white marble bathroom.

When I pinned these images onto my board, at the back of my mind I was wondering "how" I was going to make this happen. We were only just able to afford renting the living room of our current place. To be able to stay in the area and rent a flat like the one on my Vision Board felt like a bit of a pipe dream.

But, as you will soon discover through this book, our job is to get clear on what we want and allow The Universe to take care of the how. We don't always need to understand how our desires will manifest as long as we know what it is that we want. Our job is to trust that The Universe is going to provide for us, so this is what I did. I added the images to my short term Vision Board and trusted that my situation was soon to change, and change it did.

Within a few months of creating that Vision Board, I witnessed some pretty spectacular changes in my life. Not only had I quit my job to take my coaching business full time, but I'd also started earning pretty decent money through my business. However, whilst my business had begun to take off, and more money was beginning to come in, Philip and I were still living in the shared flat. We both knew it was not where we wanted to be, and so together, we made the decision that our environment needed to be upgraded.

It's important to realise that your energy dictates what you attract into your life and our living conditions certainly weren't making us feel high vibe. Your environment has a huge impact on how you feel, and since you attract based on how you feel, we knew we needed to move somewhere that made us feel amazing. So, trusting that The Universe would support us and help us find a new place to live that was within our budget, we took a leap of faith and handed in the notice on our flat.

We got to work straight away on searching for our next home but, as anyone who has ever lived in London will know, finding a place to live in a decent area without needing to sell an organ can be pretty tricky. We spent hours and hours calling up estate agents and scrolling through properties online, but we weren't having much luck. I'd forgotten how much property in our area went for once you decided to upgrade from living in the living room of a shared flat to renting a place of your own. It was depressing to be shown flat after flat that you could barely swing a cat in, yet was still five times what we were currently paying.

We had just one months notice which I'd assumed would be plenty of time to find somewhere new. As it happens, it wasn't. We had just a few days left of our lease before we needed to be out and we still hadn't found anywhere. By this point, we had packed up all of our stuff into boxes and thought we may have to put it into storage while we crashed on friends sofas for a while.

Now, the old me would have been having a total meltdown by this stage, but I'd been doing so much inner work that my faith that The Universe would pull through was unshakeable. I not only trusted that things would work out, but I expected them to.

Philip wasn't quite so convinced. In fact, he was pretty mad with himself for letting me convince him it would be a good idea to hand in our notice before we'd found somewhere else to move in to. It didn't go down particularly well either when I suggested he could meditate with my crystals to calm himself down. He told me that it was my "woo woo" crazy talk that had gotten us into this mess to begin with and that if The Universe really does "have your back", it has a funny way of showing it.

Well, as it happened, The Universe *did* have our back. A matter of days before our lease was due to end, I was coming out of our front door and I bumped into our next-door neighbour coming out of his flat. He'd bought the place months earlier and had been renovating it. I've always loved interiors and property and couldn't resist asking him if he minded me having a quick peek at the work he'd been doing. He let me into the flat so I could have a snoop around and straight away, I recognised it.

The flat looked pretty much identical to pictures of a flat I'd pinned to my vision board to showcase my short term goals. The layout was the same, the colour scheme was identical and it even had the same marble bathroom. As I walked around, there was a moment when I thought that maybe it was the exact same flat from my vision board. It wasn't, but there was no denying the uncanny resemblance.

I sort of zoned out as my neighbour waffled on about how long it had taken for the builders to finish and that the place had been in a right state when he first bought it. As his voice muffled into the background, I took a moment to imagine what it might feel like if we were about to move into this place. I pictured precisely how the living room would be arranged and exactly how my office would look. I pictured myself lounging out on our sofa, glass of wine in hand, Jo Malone candles lit, a huge bunch of white peonies on the table. I just couldn't get over how similar this place looked to the image on my vision board. Coincidence? I think not. I asked, and The Universe responded.

Only, I didn't quite have the flat in my possession. The neighbour had only just moved in so it was unlikely he'd be going anywhere soon.

"It's a beautiful place!" I told him. "You'll love living here. It's such a nice area."

"Oh, I won't be living here," he replied, my ears quickly perking up. "I'm going to be renting it out. Do you know anyone who may want to rent it?"

At this point I felt goosebumps. There I was, standing in pretty much an exact replica of the flat on my Vision Board. I even noticed the same style of mirror on the wall. The synchronicities were undeniable. This was the flat I was meant to be in. Things were working in my favour. "Me! I want to rent it!", I wanted to yell.

The one little niggle, however, was how much the flat was going to cost to rent. Sure, my business was doing well, but renting a flat like this by ourselves still seemed a bit of a push. Could we really afford it?

"Well, we could potentially be interested." I heard myself saying, trying to not give away too much and reign in my excitement. "How much were you planning on renting it for?"

He stopped for a second to think and I held my breath as he started to explain that if he didn't have to go through an agency and we were willing to move in straight away, he'd be willing to rent it to us for a lot less than the normal going rent in that area. He had business to tend to overseas and wanted to get it rented before he had to leave. He then gave me a figure, an amount that was significantly lower than what I was expecting.

"We'll take it" I told him, the words pouring out of my mouth without me really thinking. I did of course need to ask Philip his thoughts, but I knew it would be a no brainer.

Yes, it was still far more than what we were currently paying but this was The Flat and my gut told me that this was the right move. The Universe was conspiring to give me what I had asked for and was moving things in my favour. I needed to trust that The Universe would continue to support me, and my business would make more than enough for the rent to be do-able.

We moved into the flat a few days later, an easy transition given that all of our stuff was already packed into boxes and we literally just had to carry them next door.

The stars had aligned, as some may say. And, what was even more amazing, was that the money managed to figure itself out. In fact, within just a few weeks of us moving in, my business began to really take off to the point that we didn't even blink about the extra money we were now spending on rent.

This is the beauty of ASKING for what you want. If you don't ask you won't get. If you do ask, you will. The gifts of The Universe are available to you, but you need to let The Universe know that you want them and specifically what they look like. I hadn't asked The Universe for just any flat. I'd asked for a Scandi minimalist flat with a white marbled bathroom in the leafy area of Fulham at a rate that we could afford. I got exactly what I asked for. I have since heard from hundreds of my clients similar stories of their desires manifesting into physical form, stories that give me goosebumps and further cement my belief that we when we ask, The Universe will always conspire to give us what we really want.

"But what if I don't know what I want?" I hear you ask. Well, this is something many of my clients ask me, and my answer is always the same: Everyone has some sort of desire they are aware of. We all know of at least ONE thing that we want that we don't yet have in our possession. Maybe it's money, a relationship, a career. Start with that and build from there. Begin by thinking about what you already know lights you up and allow thoughts of that to fuel your excitement. Then, in that excitement, you will begin to find more and more things that bring you joy.

When you start to add things to your vision board that light you up, you begin to create forward momentum. Clarity breeds more clarity. As soon as you start mapping out one area of your life and building excitement around that, you will soon find sparks of inspiration for other areas of your life too.

So often we use the excuse of "I don't know what I want" as the reason why we don't make changes but really, we do know. We know what we want, but we are often afraid to admit it because deep down, it doesn't feel possible for us.

I spent years in jobs that didn't fulfil me under the guise of not really knowing what I should do as an alternative when really, I had a pretty solid idea of what brought me joy.

I loved being creative. I loved inspiring and helping people. I loved travelling. I loved being able to work when I wanted. I loved connecting with like-minded women. I loved reading and learning. I loved personal development. I loved writing. I loved brain-storming new ideas. Sure, I didn't know what this all meant in terms of a career path, but I knew what made me tick and it certainly wasn't being stuck in an office pushing papers under fluorescent lighting, watching the same grey suits day in day out.

If I was honest with myself, I stayed trapped in my job dissatisfaction for so long not because I didn't know what I was passionate about, but because I didn't believe bigger and better things were available to me. When I saw hugely successful women doing work that they were truly passionate about and having a lot of fun in the process, women who were travelling the globe taking their work with them, attending amazing events and working on exciting projects, I had a pang of jealousy but didn't contemplate that what they had was available for me too.

This is where Vision Boarding comes in as Vision Boarding is an opportunity to open up your horizons and to dream big. A Vision Board isn't meant to be realistic when you create it. It doesn't need to feel achievable or do-able right now. It just needs to feel exciting. Self Love is all about giving yourself permission to dream big. The only thing you need to be concerned with is "would having this make me feel good?" and if the answer is "yes", then it should and can be yours. Stick it to your board because if you can imagine it, you can achieve it.

The Universe has an infinite number of ways to help us manifest our goals and dreams and will give you subtle signs along the way of which path you should take or what decisions you should make but for now, don't worry too much how the "how" Focusing too much on the "how" is what often keeps us playing small and holds us back from daring to dream big. We get so fixated on whether things are possible for us or realistic that we create resistance towards the very things that are meant to bring us happiness.

Let's take for example a desire to manifest one million pounds. Whilst on the surface it may bring us joy, when we start to overthink things and contemplate how we will ever achieve this goal, joy and excitement can quickly turn to fear.

Our beliefs about who we are, what we are capable of, what we should do, and what we are able to attract cause us to feel doubtful about our desires. When we are in a space of doubting whether what we want is available to us, we actually hold our desires apart from us for even longer.

We will discuss the importance of your beliefs soon, but for now, I urge you to put them to one side and allow yourself to think beyond any limitations you are putting on yourself.

What would you do right now if failure wasn't an option?

Who would you be?

What would you create?

Who would you reach out to?

Where would you go?

What would you do?

Don't expect all the answers to come at once. Don't expect to get complete clarity overnight.As I said earlier, start with what you DO know that you desire and build from there. Think of your Vision Board as an ever-evolving tool, something that you keep adding to and developing.

Further into this book you will discover the importance of your beliefs and your self-worth. Once you start doing the work to change those beliefs and strengthen your self-worth, you may find that you start to think even bigger and open up your heart to even more amazing things, things that right now you perhaps aren't even giving yourself permission to consider.

Once you let go of any thoughts about, "I'm not good enough/pretty enough/smart enough/young enough/old enough etc etc" it's amazing what desires begin to surface that you'd been suppressing below the surface. Once you start to recognise that you are worthy of anything that you can imagine, it's amazing how you stop settling in life.

So many of us settle for less than what we know we deserve or less than what truly lights us up, and we do this in so many areas of our lives. We settle in jobs, in relationships, in our finances, in our health. We live by default, rather than by design, but this needn't be the case. The Universe knows no limits, and neither should you.

As one of my favourite Law of Attraction experts, Bob Proctor says, *"If you can see it in your mind, you can hold it in your hand."*

Now let's just revert back to the morning ritual I mentioned earlier and how Vision Boarding fits into this. Once you've mapped out a vision for how you want your life to look, spend some time each morning looking at that board and reminding yourself where you are heading to. Each morning, spend time getting intentional about your desires and what you really want from life.

What is important here is the feeling that you create. You will soon learn more about the importance of our energy but for now, know that you manifest into your life based on how you feel. It's not enough to just look at the board without any emotion attached. As you look at your board, you have to feel as if what you want is already yours. How would it feel if you already had the money, relationship, success, health or life that you so crave? We will go into this in more detail later into this book but showing up as if the life you want is already yours is the quickest way to receive everything you ask for.

So, we've looked at Vision Boards but what about the other parts of the morning routine? What role do these play? We will touch upon some of the other steps of the Daily Goddess Ritual further into this book. For now though, I want to focus on meditation, because a powerful tool for achieving clarity is through silence.

Listen to silence. It has so much to say ~ Rumi

Our desires speak the loudest in our moments of silence, meaning that when we turn off the mental chatter, we clear the pathways for our purpose, passions and goals to come into our awareness. Self Love is about allowing yourself time to slow down, turn inwards and ask your own inner guidance system what you really want from life.

Often, we are so busy doing and thinking, our minds one long endless to do list, that we have no room for our desires to come to light. If we can just silence the noise for even a few moments, we can allow our heart and soul to be heard, rather than our mind constantly being in the spotlight.

When people complain that they don't know what they really want, most of the time it's because they aren't listening to what their inner wisdom is telling them. We have the answers. We don't need someone else to tell us what to do, who to be or what choices to make. When you have over your life choices to another or are too heavily influenced by what others say, you disempower yourself. You have all you need within you to figure out what to do next, you just need to listen to what your higher self is telling you. The way to dial into this wisdom is through meditation.

A lot of people use meditation as a way to relieve stress or anxiety, but I've found that meditation can be as much about tuning in as it is about zoning out. When you quieten your mind, you can hear what your heart and soul is really craving. You can identify whether or not a decision is right for you.

What is also fascinating, is that in these moments where we connect with ourselves, we are also able to connect with The Universe. Meditation not only allows us to hear our own inner wisdom more clearly, but it allows us to receive messages from The Universe too. Manifesting is called "co-creating" for the reason that we are working together with The Universe to create the life we want. Whilst we must tune into our own inner guidance system to get clarity on what we should do, we also need to pay attention to what The Universe suggests too.

Think of meditation as a brainstorming session between you and The Universe where you both collaborate together on designing the life you want to live, the person you want to be and the choices you want to make. There is room for both voices to be heard, and it is through meditation that we are able to hear those voices. In moments of silence, you will not only hear your own desires more clearly, but you will also be sent subtle messages from The Universe, guiding you to the life you were meant to live.

For example, I had a client who, during a meditation session, identified that she no longer wanted to be with her current partner. She realised that it was her relationship that was holding her back and it wasn't bringing out the best in her. Her inner wisdom was telling her it was time to move on and then, out of nowhere, she saw an image of herself doing yoga in Bali.

She didn't know where this image came from, as it wasn't something she'd even thought about. She didn't even practice yoga at the time. This image wasn't coming from her own wisdom, but was a message from The Universe, a flutter of a suggestion, a gentle nudge towards the life of her dreams.

To begin with, she didn't act on this nudge. Whilst she had been doing a lot of work around trusting in The Universe and allowing herself to be guided by its messages, she was still clinging onto all of these limiting beliefs about what she should do and fears about what was possible for her. She was clinging to her comfort zone and not feeling quite ready to take chances on seemingly random messages The Universe was sending her.

Once we started to dive deeper into her beliefs and mindset however, she started to open up her mind to what other options were available to her and kept coming back to the message she'd received from The Universe.

A few months after we'd finished working together, I received a message from my client. In her email, she told me she had quit her job, moved to Bali and was training to become a Yoga teacher. Not only that, but during her first week in Bali, she'd met a guy who she really connected with and was excited to see where it would go. More recently, I had another email from her explaining she is about to host her first Yoga retreat and is now engaged to the same guy.

Let this story be a lesson to you that not all of the messages that are sent your way will make sense at first. The random flashes of inspiration or ideas that come to you during your moments of silence are often not random at all, but hints of the life you are truly destined for. Don't ignore these messages. While you may not feel ready to act on them straight away, keep a note of this guidance until you are ready to move forwards and who knows where this guidance could lead you.

That's the thing with these flashes of wisdom. We may not always feel ready to act on our urges or desires, and this is where the inner work, which we will discuss through the pages of this book comes into play. What is important is that we recognise that we have access to our desires at any given moment. When we turn off the mental chatter of our mind, allow our inner wisdom to speak up and invite The Universe into the conversation, we can find the clarity that we are searching for.

Exercise

Within the Self Love Club is an exercise called The Perfect Day. This was an exercise that helped me to get a deeper level of clarity on how I truly wanted to live my life on a daily basis.

To access the exercise, please head to: www.daniwatson.com/selfloveclub to join the Self Love Club for free.

Identifying Your Beliefs

The only limits you have, are the limits you believe
~ Wayne Dyer

Have you ever found yourself repeating certain self-sabotaging patterns of behaviour and you just can't seem to figure out why? So maybe it's finding yourself always attracting the same type of disastrous relationships. Or maybe it's repeating the same vicious cycle of debts. Or maybe you are always procrastinating on your dreams, starting something with full enthusiasm only to give it all up a few weeks later. What we do and the people, things and events we manifest into our lives are the product of what we believe about ourselves and the world around us. Our beliefs shape our reality. So often, my clients will ask me "what do I need to DO to manifest more of my desires?" My response is always the same: It's not so much about what you need to do but what you need to believe.

Once you've got clear on what you really want in life, who you want to be and how you want to feel, the next step towards cultivating endless self-love and manifesting anything you desire is to identify precisely what is holding you back right now. This is where your beliefs come under scrutiny.

If you believe you can't, chances are you probably won't. If you believe you don't deserve something, chances are you will struggle to attract it into your life. If you believe that something is difficult to obtain, such as money, chances are you will find that it will be difficult to obtain. If you believe that "all the decent men are taken" chances are all the men you meet will, in fact, be taken. You get the drift.

Negative, limiting beliefs are what keep you playing small, cause you to manifest unwanted experiences and are holds you back from living your fullest potential. Beliefs are so important and clinging onto the wrong kind of beliefs can actually hold us up from living our best lives and showing up as the best version of ourselves. Limiting beliefs can lead to us manifesting a whole host of unwanted events in our life whether it's within our finances, our health, our careers or our relationships.

Negative beliefs we hold about ourselves can also cause us to repeat the same patterns of unwanted and sometimes destructive behaviour. Whether it's an addiction to drink or drugs, compulsive shopping or overeating, a lot of the time, these behaviour patterns are triggered by our beliefs.

Belief work has played a massive role in my own journey. For much of my twenties, I had at the back of my mind some sort of vague notion of wanting to be my own boss and run my own business, but whenever this idea would raise its head, I'd quickly swat it away like I would a fly.

I had been led to believe that the best option for me was to go to University, get a "good job" and climb the career ladder until one day I retired, and so I pigeon-holed myself down this path. My beliefs had been shaped by what society, teachers and by what parents had been telling me.

Even though both of my parents had owned businesses, I also had lots of limiting beliefs around what it would take to become a successful entrepreneur. I believed you had to have some mind-blowing, never been done before business idea (not true). I believed that you had to have tonnes of cash in the bank to get your business off the ground (equally not true) and, interestingly enough, I realised I didn't believe I was "good enough" to make it. I believed I would start, only to fail (thankfully, this turned out also not to be true.)

The last belief was a funny realisation because, on paper, I'd always been "the smart one". I got good grades, went to a good University and then went on to Law School. Yet despite all of these achievement's, I didn't think I was "smart enough" to become an entrepreneur. I'd formed a belief that "school smart" wasn't the same as "business smart", which I guess is true, but for whatever reason, I'd decided that I wasn't cut out to be an entrepreneur.

As it happens, I'm not the only one who possessed this belief. I've since gone on to speak with so many brilliant women with brilliant minds who have held themselves back by their beliefs of "not being good enough".

It's Imposter Syndrome at work; the idea that no matter what you have achieved to date or how many people tell you how great or capable you are, you struggle to believe it for yourself. When you are given a promotion or witness some other sort of career or business success, you feel like a fraud and that eventually, everyone else will cotton on.

So where do these ill-founded and more often than not totally inaccurate beliefs come from? Because that's all they are really, stories that we have told ourselves or heard and we have convinced ourselves that they are true. Beliefs only exist to the extent we believe them and are often not based upon any sort of concrete facts. Instead, they have been formed because of what we've heard from others and what we've been taught by society or the people that have raised us.

This is The Law of Divine Oneness at work. Often, the beliefs we possess are not just ours, but the beliefs of those who surround us. These beliefs that we absorb from others can change the way we think and act and shape our lives for better or for worse. Basically, beliefs are a set of opinions that we've chosen to adopt as our own, often without even realising it.

This brings me to the difference between conscious and subconscious beliefs. Some beliefs we are consciously aware of. So maybe you have to spend the day listening to your inner mean girl, waffling on with her misinformed beliefs, telling you that you're not pretty/old/young/smart enough to be, do, and have anything you want in life. These are the beliefs you are aware of, the beliefs that maybe you already recognise are weighing you down and holding you back from living the life of your wildest dreams, whatever that looks like.

But then we also have hidden beliefs. These are the beliefs that are lurking deep within the subconscious that we don't even know exist. These are the dangerous beliefs because, without recognising that they exist, it becomes impossible to change them, which is the whole point of identifying beliefs in the first place.

We need to replace our unwanted, limiting beliefs with a new, more empowered set of beliefs, but to do this, we first need to have full clarity on what these unwanted beliefs actually are.

So how do we access these subconscious beliefs? Well, a good place to start is through understanding how these subconscious beliefs are initially formed. Many of our subconscious beliefs are often the beliefs that have often developed from a very early age. As children, we are like sponges. We absorb everything around us, including the beliefs of those who play a part in our life. These beliefs then become a part of us without us even realising it.

So for example, let's look at money beliefs since this is an area I've done a lot of work around and is an area where my clients find themselves holding onto a lot of limiting beliefs. Perhaps you also resonate with some of these beliefs too? Beliefs such as: Making money is hard work. Being money motivated is greedy. Money causes arguments. Being rich comes with a lot of sacrifices. Money is scarce. I'm bad at managing money.

These are just some of the beliefs my clients weren't even aware that they possessed, but when we dug into their childhood experiences around money, we realised that what they had been taught about money from their parents or other influential people in their life had affected their money beliefs.

A client of mine, Anya, remembered a childhood where her parents constantly argued about money. This had led her client to believe that "money causes arguments". Or another client, Tash, heard her Mum always tell her that "money doesn't grow on trees" and subsequently was led to believe that money is scarce. Another client was from a relatively wealthy background, but her Dad was always away with work, which created a belief that "making money comes with hard work and sacrificing your family time."

The reason why these beliefs are important is because beliefs shape your reality. So if, like my client, you believe that "money causes arguments" it's likely you will find yourself repelling money.

Money will find it hard to not only make its way into your life, but also for it to stick around.

The same principle can be applied to other areas of your life too. One of my clients was finding herself repeating the same kinds of patterns when it came to her relationships in that a great guy would come along, sweep her off her feet but she would then do something to "mess it all up". She would either cheat or just end the relationship out of the blue, and she couldn't figure out why she couldn't find someone she wanted to actually commit to.

Doing the work around her beliefs, we discovered that her Father had left at a very young age, and this led her to believe that "love leads to heartbreak". She believed that there was no point getting to close with anyone as ultimately, they would leave her anyway. She broke things off before she allowed herself to be hurt.

We repeat what we don't repair, meaning that if we want to stop seeing the same negative patterns of behaviour manifesting in our lives, we have to repair the beliefs that have caused these patterns of behaviour. Before we can do that, however, we need to understand what these beliefs actually are.

Let's start with your conscious beliefs because these are the easiest to spot. These are the constant stories that whiz through our minds on a daily basis. Remember that the first step to changing beliefs is about acknowledging what your limiting beliefs actually are, which requires you to be mindful about what your inner chitter-chatter is saying.

So often we hear our limiting beliefs, but we don't truly acknowledge them. The exercise at the end of this chapter will invite you to get intentional about what negative thought patterns keep cropping up throughout the day and actually write these things down rather than just brushing these thoughts under the carpet. Taking a belief from your mind and onto paper is an important part of the healing process. This work cannot just be done in your head, so make sure to go through this exercise properly.

For the exercise, you will be spending a full twenty-four hours where you are super intentional about what thoughts and beliefs crop up for you on a daily basis. At the end of the day, you may have a list as long as your arm of all of the negative things you are telling yourself.

You will then be asked to then think about how these beliefs may be holding you back and write these things down in your journal. If beliefs create your reality, what are the knock-on effects your beliefs are having on your own life? What choices are you making because of your beliefs? What things are you stopping yourself from doing because of your beliefs? Where are your beliefs keeping you playing small or holding yourself back from shining your light in the brightest possible way?

What you give the most attention to in your life expands, so the more you tell yourself "that's not possible for me", the more it won't be possible.

After this exercise, you should have a good understanding of some of the limiting beliefs that are preventing you from manifesting the life that you deserve, but there is still more work to do. You want to think of your mind as an iceberg. The tip of your iceberg is your conscious mind. This is the part that is visible. Below the surface, however, is where the majority of the iceberg is hidden. This submerged part of the iceberg is your subconscious mind and contains many limiting, negative beliefs, beliefs you may not even realise you possess.

Subconscious beliefs work in the same way as other thoughts we subconsciously think, such as how we think when we ride a bike. We aren't having to consciously think about every single turn of the peddle, we just do it. We ride the bike without consciously needing to think about it. This is our subconscious mind at work, and it's this subconscious mind that accounts for around 80% of our thoughts.

Subconscious beliefs operate in the same way. We believe things often without being consciously aware we believe them. Like riding a bike, to begin with, it did require conscious thought and repetition until it became subconscious. The exact is true of beliefs. For the belief to be truly adopted, it requires repetition, and evidence through further experiences for you to adopt this belief as "truth" and for it to be cemented into your subconscious.

These subconscious beliefs may be positive beliefs that serve us in our lives, but equally they can be negative and here is the interesting thing; As the mind is trying to figure out whether or not a belief is "true" through repetition or evidence that backs up that belief, in the meantime, it will automatically adopt the "negative" belief. We are hardwired to give an event a negative meaning over a positive one. This is known as negative brain bias.

Now you may be thinking "that sounds like Mother Nature playing a cruel trick", but negative brain bias was actually meant as a way to protect us thousands of years ago when we were constantly being threatened by our environment and the things within it. To survive against threats of attack, we needed to be able to retain negative thoughts so we could learn from our mistakes. Although we have now evolved and no longer require the same sort of survival mechanisms, the brain still focuses on the negative thoughts and negative bias still exists.

When I first learned about negative bias, it was a bit of a breakthrough for me. Suddenly, a lot of things made a lot of sense, particularly in relation to my own feelings of low self-worth. What I realised was that I wasn't to blame for the negative thoughts and feelings I had about myself. It wasn't my fault that I had adopted my limiting beliefs as all humans are hardwired to adopt the negative thoughts.

What I've since learned is that while we are hardwired to adopt negative thoughts, we can rewire our brains and train them to adopt a new, positive belief system. We have the power to change our negative beliefs, rewrite our story and reprogram our mind so that we create a reality that we love. How we do this is something I will get to within the next chapter, but for now, we need to look at how to identify these hidden beliefs. This requires us to examine where these hidden beliefs originate.

Where do most of our limiting beliefs come from? Well, the majority of these beliefs are formed in early childhood when we are like sponges, soaking up everything we hear and experience around us. Then, over time, these beliefs are backed up by further evidence, and unless they are challenged and nipped in the bud, we eventually adopt these beliefs as the truth.

Once we do this, we then continue to look for evidence to support these beliefs. Our minds actively seek out experiences that help reinforce that belief. We then begin to act in a way that confirms that belief until eventually, the belief becomes a part of who we are, deeply entrenched in our minds and affecting our choices, what we say and how we show up without us even realising.

If the beliefs we have adopted are negative, they can have a whole host of negative impact on our reality. Remember; your beliefs create your reality, and, as one of my favourite childhood authors Roald Dahl once famously said, *"If you don't believe in magic, rarely will you find it."*

So let's say you believe deep down you are not worthy of love, rarely will you find love. If you don't believe you are capable of being wealthy, rarely will you find wealth. If you don't believe you are capable of being successful, rarely will you find success.

If your belief was first installed at a very early age, your young mind won't have been able to have made sense of it properly. Children are particularly egocentric and tend to think everything revolves around them, and the same is true of their beliefs. Rather than having the ability to experience an event and evaluate it as something that has happened to them, often they will interpret it as something that has happened because of them. As a result, the experience can trigger a new belief about themselves.

So, for example, I had a client who remembered a time in her childhood when they had to submit a project at school. Some of the children in her class were rewarded with these special badges for their work. My client had spent ages on this project and was really proud of it so was incredibly upset when she wasn't awarded one of the special badges. Rather than thinking about this in a logical way ("there are only a few badges to go out, and it was just a matter of the teacher's preference as to who received them"), my client instead felt hurt, stupid and not good enough.

Subsequently, she developed a belief that "I'm not good enough". A large proportion of our negative, deeply rooted subconscious beliefs originate from our childhood, which is why a big part of the work I do with my own clients is to invite them to trace back to earlier experiences and events to help them to pinpoint where the belief was first adopted.

One exercise I invite my clients to do is to think about what events or experiences they remember from their childhood that could have impacted their current belief system. Do they remember experiencing something particularly negative or traumatic? What were some of the things they were taught as a child? What phrases do they remember hearing? Below are some of the events my clients have identified that have had a knock-on impact on their belief system:

A parent leaving or parents splitting up.
Being picked on at school.
Getting told off by a teacher for something they didn't do.
A new sibling arriving and parents giving more attention to a new brother/sister.
Being told that you're not "smart enough"
Receiving a bad grade at school.
Not getting picked for a role in the school play.
Parents arguing about money.

Once they've identified a significant moment, I then invite them to think about how that made them feel, what meaning they gave to that experience and subsequently, what belief do they think they may have adopted as a result.

So for example, a client of mine, Erin, remembered a time when she was younger and being looked after by her Aunt. Going back into this memory, she recalled how she'd wanted to perform a dance show for her Aunt. Erin had loved dancing and singing as a child, and was always looking for an opportunity to entertain her family. Her Aunt however, was not quite so keen on the idea and told Erin that she was being too loud and that "no-one likes a show off". This remark stuck with Erin.

She remembered how she felt embarrassed about wanting to dance, something she had always felt she was good at and enjoyed. Her Aunt's words had made her feel like she was being a nuisance, and Erin felt rejected by this experience. Now, while her Aunt's words in isolation may not have caused a limiting belief to form, it certainly planted the seed.

When Erin and I found ourselves working together years later, something she told me she was really struggling with was showing up within her business. She had recently become a coach and, in order to attract clients, needed to get visible online so that the people who needed her coaching could actually find her. Erin had huge amounts of resistance towards this.

Despite knowing that what she wanted to offer could really help others, her fears were keeping her paralysed from taking action. As we started to do the inner work to dig into what she was really afraid of, we arrived at the memory of her visit to her Aunts. Remembering this event, my client realised she had attached a meaning to this experience, and that meaning was "I am not worthy of being seen."

Erin then went on to recall other memories that had subsequently reinforced this belief. For example, Erin remembered a later experience where she auditioned for the part in a school play but didn't get the lead as she hoped. Rather than her mind trying to find some logical answer to why she didn't get the part ("someone else was better suited for the part that had years of acting experience") her mind took the experience as further evidence to support the belief "I'm not worthy of being seen".

What subsequent experiences are you able to identify in your own life that reinforce that first, negative belief? Every time that belief is reinforced, it becomes more powerful until it gets to the stage where you believe it to be the truth.

These beliefs may be first encountered through our own experiences, but equally they can be beliefs that we absorb from the people who raise us. For example, a huge part of my own personal and spiritual journey has been my relationship with money. When I started doing work on my money mindset, one of the things I needed to do was to identify my own subconscious limiting money beliefs, and many of these I realised had been formed in childhood.

I had seen my parents act a certain way around money and then repeated these patterns of behaviour in my own life. Seeing my Dad "work hard" for his money led me to adopt his belief that making money is hard work, and subsequently, I found myself hitting burn out in order to make money.

Think about what beliefs you may have adopted from the people who played a significant role in your upbringing. It could be a parent, a sibling or a teacher. What things did you hear them say which you've now adopted into your own belief system? How have you found yourself repeating the same patterns of behaviour and what underlying belief does this behaviour point to? Then, what did you subsequently hear or what did you later experience to reinforce this belief?

So for me and my money story, I identified my teachers telling me at school that I'd need to work really hard if I wanted to get a good job that paid well, reinforcing that "making money is hard work".I then experienced life working in the City where everyone wore "working hard" like a badge of honour. It was working late and coming into the office on a weekend that rewarded you with a promotion and a pay rise. Again, this reinforced my beliefs that "making money is hard work"

To help you figure out what experiences have further supported your belief, go back in your life and identify specific moments where you felt your deep-rooted belief. So let's say you've identified a belief that "I'm not loveable", can you remember a number of specific times when you felt this way? Take your journal and sit with this belief and try and come up with as many circumstances as possible that are evidence to support this belief.

As you find more and more evidence from your experiences to support your limiting belief, you will soon realise it's no wonder this belief is so deeply entrenched and why you believe this belief so strongly that your mind has declared it as truth. These deep-rooted beliefs have a knock-on effect on what you think, how you feel how you act and then subsequently, what you manifest into your life. If the deep-rooted belief is negative, this then leads to negative thoughts, feelings, actions and manifestations.

So in the case of my client who identified the deep-rooted belief of ""I'm not worthy of being seen", this fuelled feelings of worthlessness and low confidence. These feelings then triggered her to hold herself back when it came to her business. She struggled to promote herself, selling herself and subsequently, was ready to throw the towel in completely as her business wasn't generating any income. Her deep-rooted belief had led to a lack of clients and therefore a lack of money, and therefore her business wasn't growing in the way she'd hoped it would. Her belief had caused her to manifest a negative experience in her life.

When I first began to dive into my own subconscious mind, so much began to make sense to me, and I began to understand why I had attracted certain people and experiences into my life. As much as it was a bitter pill to swallow, my beliefs had been creating much of my reality. The job, the debts, the relationship. Everything I was manifesting could be traced back to something within my subconscious belief system.

Whether I realised or not, my inner world had been shaping my reality. My beliefs about myself, what I was worth, what I was capable of, what was expected of me, and what I deserved had caused me to manifest a lot of unwanted experiences into my life. As tough as this was to realise, it also felt quite empowering. If my negative beliefs were the cause of my current circumstances, I knew that if I ditched any beliefs that no longer served me or the life I wanted to create, I had the power to completely turn my world around.

This is the beauty of mindset work. When you become intentional on what is going on in your inner world, you can consciously create a new reality in your physical world. We have a choice over the thoughts we think and the beliefs we possess, and because of this, we have a choice about the life we want to live, the people we want to attract, the work we do and how we spend our time.

We can make a choice to let go of the beliefs that hold us back, even those beliefs that are deeply entrenched in our subconscious. With knowledge comes power. When you know what your unwanted beliefs are, you then have the power to change them. By changing your perception of the experience that helped form the belief and all of the evidence that reinforced that belief, you can transform that deeply rooted core belief and replace it with something more empowering.

We will explore transforming beliefs in the next chapter but for now, take some time to go through the exercises below so that you can identify any beliefs you currently possess that are stopping you from living your life in the fullest possible way.

Exercise One: Twenty Four Hours To Monitor Your Beliefs

Take your journal and a pen and keep these with you throughout your day. Spend a whole 24 hours keeping a note of any beliefs that crop up for you and writing them down.

Every time a thought pops into your head, identify whether this is a limiting belief and write it down.

Leave a space of about half a page under each belief for the next part of this exercise. After the 24 hour period, once you have your list of negative beliefs, write underneath each belief how it may be holding you back.

So let's say you wrote down "I'm not smart enough", underneath this belief you would write down all of the ways in which this belief has held you back in the past, all of the ways in which this holding you back right now and all of the ways in which this belief will hold you back in the future.

For example:

Limiting belief = "I'm not smart enough"

How this has held me back in the past = Not going for the job I really wanted.

How this is holding me back now = Not putting myself forward for promotion.

How this will hold me back in the future = Will prevent me from starting the business I would love to create.

Exercise Two - Identifying Subconscious Beliefs:

Part One: Your childhood experiences

Do you remember experiencing something particularly negative or traumatic? If so, write down this memory. What belief do you think you may have adopted as a result of this experience? Write it down. What subsequent experiences are you able to identify in your own life that reinforce that first, negative belief? Write these down too.

Part Two: What you were taught by or heard from those who raised you?

Think about a certain area of your life where you have created a reality that doesn't match the reality you would like to create. For example, it could be in your finances; it could be relationships; it could be health, it could be in your career.

With that specific topic in mind, what do you remember being taught about that particular topic from your parents, teachers, or anyone else who raised you? What do you remember hearing others say in relation to that topic? What experiences do you remember having in relation to that specific topic?

Write these things down, then ask yourself what kind of belief may have been formed through absorbing these lessons and words of others.

Part Three: What subsequent experiences reinforced these beliefs?

Thinking about the beliefs you have identified in parts one and two, go through your life in chronological order and write down any of the experiences that may have backed up and reinforced those beliefs. What events can you remember that validated the initial belief?

Transforming Your Beliefs.

Everything that happens to you is a reflection of what you believe about yourself. We cannot outperform our level of self -esteem. ~ Iyanla Vanzant

It may come as a bit of a shock to the system to realise that you and your own beliefs have shaped your reality, but with that knowledge comes power and the ability to change your beliefs so that they help you to live life in your fullest, most brilliant way possible.

The good news about beliefs is that they can be changed. Beliefs aren't facts. They are subjective, a matter of opinion, but they can become facts if we cling to the belief tightly enough and allow ourselves to be guided by them. The longer we hold onto a belief and the more we find evidence to back it up, the more powerful that belief will become. The more we reiterate a belief over and over to ourselves each day, the more we strengthen that belief.

Now, this is great if we are talking about positive beliefs such as "I'm a total badass that is amazing at everything, and all that I touch turns to gold, and Ryan Gosling wants to marry me I'm just that amazing. I'm so amazing that Ed Sheeran wrote a song about me. Yep, I'm incredible."

Unfortunately, many of the beliefs we do affirm to ourselves on a daily basis are not always the most positive ones. From the exercise within the previous chapter, where you made an observation of your beliefs and thoughts that popped into your head, how many of those were positive in comparison to how many were negative?

My guess is that there were a lot of unwanted beliefs that came up for you, in which case, it's time to change those beliefs and replace them with a new set of beliefs that match the reality we want to create for yourself.

Imagine if you believed without any shadow of a doubt that failure wasn't an option, that whatever you put your mind to, you would be a success at. What would you do?

Or, imagine if you believed with every inch of your being that today was the day you were going to meet your soulmate. How would you show up differently?

Or, let's say you believe wholeheartedly that within the next few years, you are going to be a multi-millionaire. What leap of faith would you take right now to set the wheels in motion?

The thing is, whatever we believe about our future, we can never say with 100% certainty if it is true, unless of course we have been born with psychic powers. So why not then choose to adopt beliefs that are empowering and that make us feel good, beliefs that give us courage to do the things we've always wanted, rather than holding us back?

Sometimes, we cling to our limiting beliefs so tightly that we actually believe them to be 100% true, even if they are beliefs that have yet to manifest. I know a lot of women who have taken the belief "I will fail as an entrepreneur" as gospel so incidentally, they fail by default. They fail because they don't even give themselves an option to even try to succeed. They are so committed to their belief that things will not work out and have convinced themselves that this belief is the truth, that they give up before they even give themselves a chance to start.

So many of us are guilty of this. We hold these beliefs up on a pedestal and let them dictate our life as if we are certain that these beliefs are solid facts. If we can do this with negative beliefs, if we can hold up these limiting beliefs about what we are capable of to be true, why can't we do the same with positive ones also?

What is to stop us from choosing a set of beliefs that support our goals and adopting these beliefs instead? If our beliefs become self fulfilling prophecies, we should and indeed can choose beliefs that shape our future for the better and encourage us to become the women we are meant to be and do the things we are meant to do.

Let's look at how we change our beliefs or let go of the beliefs that aren't serving us and create for ourselves a new, more empowering set of beliefs that matches the reality we want to create for ourselves.

Firstly, I want you to realise that in any experience you have, you have a choice over how you perceive that experience and how you react to it. You have a choice about how you now think about certain experiences that have happened to you in your past that have shaped your beliefs and your life to date.

So let's say you possess the belief "I'm not worthy of love" that developed because your Father left at a young age. When that experience happened during your childhood, you didn't yet have the emotional maturity to properly process and evaluate the experience.

At the time, the experience made you feel like it was your fault. Children are ego-centric. They think the world revolves around them and subsequently, when they experience something negative, they will perceive it to be "their fault" and therefore adopt a belief about themselves e.g. "I'm not worthy of love." As adults however, we can re-evaluate an experience and change how we perceive it.

So for example, a client of mine who would continuously sabotage relationships with kind, loving guys who treated her well, had a deep rooted belief that she was "not worthy of love," because of her father leaving at about the age of six. At the time, her child mind made this event about her. She perceived it to be her fault and therefore developed this limiting belief about who she was and her self worth.

But, as an adult, she now had a choice about how she could perceive that event and give it a different meaning. Rather than viewing her father leaving as an event that she was to blame for, she was able to re-frame the experience. So in my clients case, she realised that her Father and Mother had been arguing a lot, her father had a lot of pressure from his work and he had also never really gotten over the death of his own Father, who had passed away before he'd had a chance to make peace with him. Once this event had been given a new explanation, we then had to work through every other piece of evidence that had reinforced the belief and give it a new meaning also.

One technique I love to use to help my clients through this process is an NLP technique called re-imprinting. It's a technique where I take my clients through memories of past events and give them a new meaning. Something you can do right now though, is to take any past experiences that have helped create or reinforce one of your limiting beliefs and ask yourself: How can I look at this experience differently so that it becomes nothing to do with me or my worth?

So let's take my client who wasn't given a "special badge" for her school project, which triggered the belief "I'm not good enough" How could my client look at this experience differently so that it becomes nothing to do with her? Well, she could conclude that the teacher didn't have time to properly read through every project and therefore just had to assign badges at random. She could conclude that the teacher favoured the underdog and wanted to give badges to those who she felt needed more reassurance.

Go through some of your own experiences that have either triggered or reinforced a limiting belief. What new meaning could you give to these experiences that had nothing to do with you? How can you take yourself out of the picture?

In order to change beliefs, we need to challenge them. Our minds have been so focused on finding evidence to back up our beliefs but now it's time to change that and start crushing those beliefs that have been holding us back. We can do this not just in relation to old experiences, but any other experience we have moving forwards.

So let's say you get ghosted by a guy you are seeing. You could choose to make this all about you, reinforcing a belief of "I'm not loveable/pretty enough/good enough/worthy of love." The more empowering approach however, would be to take yourself out of the picture entirely ("he's got commitment issues/he's not ready for a relationship/he's stressed from work/he's not the right guy for me")

Whilst you can't change your past, you do have the power to change the narrative. You can choose how to tell the stories from your history. You can also choose how you write your current and future chapters.

Another thing to be mindful of is the underlying positive benefit of an unwanted belief. One of things I learned about when I was completing my training as a Theta Healer, a technique that involves removing unwanted beliefs, is that sometimes, we hold onto a limiting belief because it serves us in some way. A negative belief may have some knock-on benefit, and because of this benefit, we cling to the belief.

So let's say you believe that "I'm not smart enough to start a business" In what way may this have a positive benefit? Well, if you convince yourself that "I'm not smart enough to start a business" it means that you have a good excuse for not even trying. You don't have to step out of your comfort zone. You don't have to open yourself up to failure or criticism. The belief protects you. But the same belief also keeps you playing small. The same belief can hold you back from creating the life you really want, doing the things you were meant to do and being the woman you were meant to be.

A lot of negative beliefs will come with some sort of benefit. The trick is to weigh up the benefit of holding onto that belief versus the benefit of letting it go. Sure it may feel safe to stay where you are, but how would that feel five years from now? Ten years from now? Would you be okay never taking that leap and always wondering "what if?" How would you feel if someone close to you took that leap and you had to witness their success from the sidelines?

Change is always scary, but you know what's scarier? Regret. On the surface, it may seem easier to cling onto a limiting belief and protect ourselves, but once we way up both sides of the coin, it may be evident that the cost of that limiting belief far outweighs any perceived benefits.

Another example of how a limiting belief can serve you so that you cling onto it, is from a client of mine called Ria. She realised she had a money belief that she just couldn't shift. The belief was "I'm no good with managing my money." What we realised was that holding onto this limiting belief was actually serving her in that she could avoid taking financial responsibility.

Her partner handled all of the finances and did all of the boring stuff such as pay the bills and taxes. She didn't need to get involved in any of it because she believed "she was no good with managing money" What she didn't realise however was that this belief was in fact causing her to resist money in her life. She was struggling to manifest money into her business because she was essentially saying to The Universe "I can't handle money!" And what do you think happens when you say you can't handle something? Do you invite it in with open arms? Are you ready to receive it? Of course not! You repel it. You reject it. The Universe recognises your belief and thinks "you can't handle money" therefore won't send you any more of it.

This is the thing about beliefs. The Universe doesn't distinguish between "good" and "bad". It simply responds to whatever messages we are telling it and if your subconscious mind is saying "I can't handle money!" you are likely to manifest a lack of money in your life.

In order to help my client replace this belief, we not only had to identify its source and give that a new meaning, we also needed to find every other piece of evidence that had reinforced that belief and give it a new meaning too.

Next, we had to detach the belief from the positive benefit of not having to take part in taxes. We achieved this through re-framing the supposedly "positive benefit" of holding onto the belief and recognising that it wasn't perhaps a benefit after all. Whilst it may not be fun to pay taxes and getting out of that task may seem like a bonus, actively engaging with your finances gives you financial responsibility. By taking care of your bills, you are showing The Universe that you are in control of your money and therefore The Universe will be eager to send you more.

We also looked at the negative connotations she gave to paying taxes. Rather than seeing tax as a negative thing, we reframed it into something positive. Paying taxes meant she was contributing to society. The roads she drives on, the healthcare she is provided with and the schools her children are sent to can only exist because of taxes, taxes that she has paid.

We also looked at ways in which we could make the task of managing her money, taxes and bills feel more fun and empowering her. This is something that I urge you to do if money is one of the areas of your life that you want to change and have recognised that you are perhaps brushing things under the carpet when it comes to your finances. I want you to take charge of your money and have fun doing so because the more you resist taking financial responsibility, the more you signal to The Universe that you are not able to handle more money if it were to show up in your life.

This had been my experience with money for much of my twenties. Rather than face up to my debts, I would instead literally brush my debts under the carpet in that I hid all of my unopened statements under my bed, pretending like they didn't exist.

The thought of tackling my finances and getting clarity on my current situation gave me knots in my stomach. I clung to my belief "I'm bad with money" as doing so meant I had an excuse for why I wasn't getting on top of my money. I knew however, that if I was to receive money with ease and flow, I'd have to show The Universe I was "good with money".

I set a time aside in my schedule to face up to my finances and to do an audit of what was going in and out of my life each month and the extent of my debts. To make the experience feel as positive as possible, I dressed in an outfit that made me feel confident and empowered, I poured myself a glass of wine, lit a few scented candles and had a "date night" with my finances.

This is something I instructed my client to also do, and by turning the task of managing her finances into a more positive experience, it helped her to stop clinging to the belief "I'm bad with money" and enabled her to adopt a new belief "I'm excellent at managing money" so that subsequently, she could manifest more of it. Dressing in her favourite dress, pouring herself a glass of her favourite wine and putting on her favourite music, she finally got down and dirty with her finances once and for all.

The result? She turned something she'd been dreading into this hugely uplifting experience, got organised with her monthly accounts and subsequently, showed The Universe that she could handle money.

Think about your own limiting beliefs. How could your limiting beliefs be serving you in some way? How could your negative beliefs be providing you with some sort of benefit? Once you've recognised the benefit, how can you change the way you perceive this benefit so that it's no longer a benefit at all?

Deconstructing beliefs by changing the way we perceive the experiences that have helped form our beliefs or the experiences that reinforced the belief, can help us rid ourselves of limiting beliefs we have been holding onto, but what about programming our brain with a new, more empowered set of beliefs?

In order to manifest what we desire, our beliefs have to match those desires. We therefore not only need to rid ourselves of negative beliefs, but we also need to create new beliefs that match the reality we want to create. Our beliefs have to be aligned with the version of ourselves who already has all that we desire. What does the woman who already has what you desire believe?

- The woman who has attracted a deeply loving and healthy relationship with the man of her dreams believes she is worthy of love.
- The woman who has created a huge amount of success for herself believes she deserves success.
- The woman who manifests money with ease believes she is worthy of receiving money.

Your beliefs will always match your reality. So if you want to manifest love, you have to believe you are loveable. If you want to manifest wealth, you have to believe you are worthy of and capable of being wealthy.

Creating a new set of beliefs is something I do with my clients. Many of my clients have the desire to become a super successful and abundant entrepreneur, running their business with ease and flow. One exercise I invite them to do is to ask themselves: What does the version of you who already is that super successful and abundant entrepreneur believe?

These are some of the common beliefs that come up:

- She believes she is confident.
- She believes she is worthy of success.
- She believes she is worthy of wealth.
- She believes she is capable of being a successful entrepreneur.
- She believes she is amazing at what she does. She believes that her success is non-negotiable.
- She believes she is worthy of investing in herself and her business.
- She believes that making money is easy.
- She believes that clients are willing to pay her what she is worth.

Once we have established what beliefs you need to possess to create the reality you want, the next step is to reprogram the mind to adopt these beliefs as your new truth. One simple way to do this is through affirmations. Taking the beliefs of the version of you who has already manifested the things you desire, how can you turn those beliefs into a positive affirmation?

Going back to the morning ritual I described earlier in this book, affirmations are a powerful way to help you reprogram your mind with a new, more empowered set of beliefs. The issue for many people, however, is that they simply cannot get affirmations to work for them. I have worked with so many women who have been used affirmations with zero effect and normally, this comes down to a few reasons:

Firstly, they struggle to create lasting changes in their beliefs because they have not been consistent enough with affirmations. Affirmations are not something you can use a handful of times and expect them to undo years of subconscious programming. Affirmations do take time, time which many people aren't prepared to commit.

The second thing is that from my experience, affirmations alone are not enough. They have certainly helped hugely within my own mindset work, and to this day, affirmations are still a part of my morning ritual, but they normally need to be backed up by other coaching techniques or spiritual practices too.

Whilst I firmly believe in the power of affirmations and know that saying out loud positive affirmations as part of my morning routine has been a game-changer for my life, I've also used lots of other techniques to help transform beliefs to reinforce the work of affirmations.

The third thing, and this is important, is that when people repeat affirmations that they do not truly believe or that are even the opposite of what they truly believe, the subconscious mind will sometimes reject these affirmations and actually become more resistant to the new belief and more stressed as a result. So in this way, the wrong affirmations really can do more harm than good.

Affirmations can actually be more harm than good when people simply repeat the complete opposite of what they think. When you are so far removed from the words that you are saying, the mind has a hard time adopting that belief as your own. This is why generalised affirmations such as "I am the most beautiful woman in the world" or "I am incredibly wealthy" do not always work. If that belief is so far off from how that person actually feels about themselves, their subconscious mind will try and fight to resist this affirmation, and the result would be more stress without any positive change.

When I first started using affirmations, one area of my life I wanted to change was my finances. I read a book on money mindset that told me to stand in front of the mirror each morning and say to myself "I am an incredibly wealthy multi millionaire."

I started to do this each day, but something didn't feel right. In fact, I felt I had a huge amount of resistance to these words. At the time, I was in a lot of debt and I hadn't yet started my business. The words I was saying seemed too far removed from my current situation for them to be believable. I had no clue how I was going to pay off my debts, let alone make millions given that I wasn't getting paid millions by my job.

I didn't understand how that affirmation could ever become my new truth given what my situation was at the time. My mind, therefore, wanted to reject this statement. It got to a point where I began to give up on affirmations as I didn't feel like they were having much of an effect.

What I later realised, however, was that it wasn't that affirmations don't work. It was simply that I wasn't using them in the right way. The key is to use affirmations that feel carry some degree of belief to the person saying them. The affirmation should repeat something positive that a person already believes to be true, or that someone believes could become true in the future.

So for example, for someone who is struggling with beliefs about their appearance: I am beautiful enough, or I am beautiful inside and out may work better than I am the most beautiful woman in the world.

Or, for someone like myself who was trying to manifest wealth and at that time was totally broke, *"My money is increasing daily"*, worked better than *"I am an incredibly wealthy multi millionaire."* Rather than stating My life is perfect in every way as it is, a more realistic option would be My life is becoming better, or I am working towards a better life.

These minor distinctions are very significant to the subconscious mind. Remember that as your mindset expands, so too will your affirmations. Whilst right now, I am a millionaire may actually create more resistance for you, in time, this may start to feel believable for you.

Exercise - Create Your Affirmations

To create your own set of daily affirmations, take a piece of paper and divide it into three columns. In column one, start by taking all of the negative beliefs you have identified so far and write them down on the left-hand side of a piece of paper.

Then, for each belief, ask yourself "what alternate, more empowering belief would the higher version of me adopt? What would the version of me who already has all of my desires believe?"

Write the answer down in column two next to the belief.

This would be the belief you are working towards.

Right now, this belief may feel completely alien to you. It may feel so far removed from your current reality that you have a hard time feeling like this belief could ever be true.

If this is the case, then in column three, I want you to write down a belief that feels good to you right now.

This should be something that you either have a tiny shred of belief about already, or is something that you feel you could believe to be true in the future.

It shouldn't feel so out of reach that your mind rejects it entirely. So for example, let's say in column one you identified a belief of "I'm not good enough to be successful".

In column two, (What would the version of me who already has all of my desires believe?) you may put "she is incredibly confident in her abilities and believes she is amazing at what she does."

In column three, you should write down something that you believe right now about yourself that aligns with the higher version of you.

This should be something that you either believe to be true or is something you feel could be true in the future. So here, the belief could be "I am building up my knowledge each day and every day I'm getting more confident."

What you wrote in column three will then become your new positive affirmation to repeat to yourself each day.

In time, you may come back to the third column and change it so that it gradually starts to align with whatever you wrote down in column two.

As you strengthen your beliefs about yourself and the world around you, you will find that adopting the beliefs of the higher version of you who already has everything you desire, becomes easier. There will be less resistance towards these beliefs as you start to uplevel your own mindset.

Consistency is key here. The daily repetition of these new beliefs helps to lock the belief in at the subconscious level. The more consistent you are with saying these affirmations on a daily basis, the more your brain habituates these statements and believes them to be true. Soon enough, these statements will form a belief so strong that you believe it to be true to your core and the belief will become a part of you without you even consciously being aware of it.

In the same way negative subconscious beliefs can cause you to self sabotage and repeat the same destructive patterns of behaviour, keep you playing small or hold you back from reaching your fullest potential, subconscious positive beliefs can have the total opposite effect.

If you subconsciously believe you are an empowered, successful and abundant goddess who has Beyoncé levels of confidence and everything she touches turns to gold, you show up as that person without even needing to think about it. And, if this is the case, what kinds of things do you think you may be able to achieve as a result? What would you do? What would you create? What chances would you take? What kinds of things do you think you'd be able to manifest into your world? Our beliefs can be the making or the breaking of us.

Fortunately, we have the power to choose which beliefs we adopt and, if consistent with the belief work, we can program our minds with a set of beliefs that allow us to be, do and have anything our heart desires.

If you believe that The One is just about to walk into your life, he will.

If you believe wholeheartedly in your own success, you will achieve it.

If you believe that riches are coming your way, you'll find wealth starts showing up.

If you believe with every inch of your being that you are an inspiring and impactful leader, you will indeed inspire the masses.

Getting what we want is not just what we do, but what we believe about ourselves. Our desires start with our beliefs, so isn't about time you make yours work for you rather than against you?

Aside from affirmations, there are a whole host of other tools that I love to use with my clients to help them shift beliefs. NLP and EFT are both incredibly powerful for changing beliefs. In fact, I've conducted NLP sessions where beliefs have been changed in just one session. For some of the more stubborn beliefs, it can take a number of different techniques to really change beliefs for good.

One ritual that I find a lot of my clients love for belief work is meditation. We've already looked at how meditation can help you get clear on what you want, but what many people don't realise is that meditation is also incredible for transforming even the most stubborn of beliefs.

Not many people associate meditation with belief work. Instead, they view it as a tool for relaxing, relieving anxiety or connecting with their intuition. Meditation can however work wonders on beliefs given that most beliefs are formed at an early age when our brain operates mainly in theta brain waves.

It's whilst operating in a theta state that our brain is the most impressionable, which is why children are like sponges. Coming into a theta brain wave through meditation, we can actually rewire our subconscious beliefs with new, more empowering beliefs.

In The Self Love Club, you will be able to access positive affirmation guided meditations using theta waves to help you program your mind with more positive beliefs. Please visit www.daniwatson.com/theselfloveclub to join for free.

Whilst we are on the topic of negative beliefs, let take some time to think about fear, because fears, if given enough fuel, can often turn into beliefs. A lot of my clients come to me with fear based beliefs such as "I believe I will fail" or "I believe that I will spend money and I won't make it back" or "I believe that I will ask this guy on a date and he will reject me."

Fears and beliefs go hand in hand. A fear can emerge, sometimes without any real logic behind it and, given enough attention, can become a belief. Just as we can positively affirm things in our mind through positive affirmations, we can also negatively affirm things too through our fears.

If you are constantly worrying about things not working out, fearing the worst and scared of failing, over time, these thoughts can turn into beliefs, beliefs which we then hold so strongly that they are not up for negotiation. These beliefs then proceed to dictate our lives, holding us back every day in a number of different ways.But if we stop our fears in their tracks, we can also stop the belief from forming in the first place.

One of my favourite books I've read on my spiritual journey is *"A Return To Love"* by Marrianne Williamson. In this book, she shares how miracles occur when we change our perception from fear, to love. By choosing love over fear, you stop fear-based beliefs in their tracks and open yourself up to the most abundant, successful, delicious life possible.

So many of us are guilty of being more committed to our fears than we are to our dreams. We put our fears on a pedestal, giving them far more credit than they're due. We blow our fears out of proportion, exaggerating them to be far bigger than they need to be. We create fear-based scenarios in our minds, imagining the worst rather than expecting the best. Fear is often our default setting.

Think about your goals for a second. Think about those big, lofty goals, the goals that perhaps right now still feel a little (or perhaps a lot) out of your reach. What is the feeling that comes up when you think about that goal? Is it excitement? Or is it fear? Maybe it's a mixture of both, but I'd say that in 99% of cases, fear will be present. If fear isn't present, chances are you'd have already achieved your goal already.

Your fears may show up in a number of different ways. It may be a fear of failure, a fear of rejection, a fear of putting yourself out there, a fear of losing money, a fear of responsibility, a fear of success. These fears, if given enough attention, become beliefs which then become reality. But, when you choose love over fear, miracles occur. In any given situation you can be guided by fear or led by love. With every experience you face, you can ask yourself "how would I respond or act right now if I was being led by love?"

Let me show you how this may work in practice by sharing with you how I was able to choose love over fear and as a result, went on to create a life of passion, purpose and abundance.

During much of my twenties, a lot of the choices I made were through fear. I chose jobs based on what felt like the safest rather than what really lit me up. I chose to stay in a relationship because I was afraid of being alone. I was drinking far too much to numb my anxiety from my job and relationship because I was too afraid of facing up to things and making scary changes.

Fear based thoughts led to fear based actions, thus reinforcing fear based beliefs such as "I will fail", "I'm not worthy of love" and "I'm incapable of dealing with my emotions" How could I have chosen love over fear in these situations? I could have chosen to do what I love and followed my passions. I could have loved myself enough to walk away. I could have recognised that my body needed love and filled it with things that nourished me.

See how our lives can be altered for the better when we commit to love over fear? These actions based out of love then lead to beliefs based out of love. I can be successful doing what I love. I can be successful doing what I love. I am worthy of loveI am healthy and vibrant and make empowered choices for my body. These beliefs then shape our reality. We become successful doing what we love. We attract love into our lives. We become the healthiest versions of ourselves.

When I realised how committed I had been to my fears, I realised these fears had been strengthening my fear based beliefs and therefore creating a fear based reality I knew deep down did not serve me. In turning to love, I was able to then manifest some profound changes in my life. I found my soulmate, I started my business, I began a regular yoga practice and started to become incredibly mindful of what I was eating, my finances dramatically increased and I developed new relationships with some incredibly inspiring women.

Probably my biggest shift away from fear was in terms of my career. Every single choice I'd made for my career up until the day I started my business was a fear-based choice. I studied Law not because I loved the subject, but because I feared not having financial security and feared to be seen as "unsuccessful". It felt like the safe option. I stayed in jobs that left me unfulfilled because I was scared of starting something new that could potentially fail. If I'd chosen to act from a place of love sooner, who knows how far I'd have taken my business by now.

Regret I didn't start things sooner though isn't something I choose to dwell on. Regret is a waste of energy, but not only that, I firmly believe we grow through what we go through and that sometimes, we have to experience things in order to find out who we really are and what we really want.

When I finally started my business, for the first time in a long time, I was making a decision for myself. I was choosing a path because I knew it would bring me joy, rather than making decisions based upon what I felt I should do. For the first time in a while, I was choosing love over fear. At the time, I wasn't conscious of this, but now, it makes so much sense and explains why things took off so quickly.

When you are guided by love over fear, The Universe has no choice but to support you. As I launched my business, my only concern was following my passion. At the time, I wasn't even really thinking about the money. In fact, I still wasn't entirely convinced how profitable a coaching career could be. Sure, I'd seen a lot of other women create 6, 7 and even 8 figure businesses in the coaching world but a part of me still wasn't sure if this was possible for me (I guess at this point I still had a lot of work to do around my beliefs!)

I leapt into my business, driven by my desire to be of service and to help others live their fullest, most brilliant and abundant lives possible. It was the excitement of seeing other women experience the same kinds of inner shifts I had which spurred me on. The thought of being a source of inspiration to others and helping them shine their brightest possible light got me lit up like a Christmas tree.

I was also so excited to create. Writing content, developing my brand aesthetics, planning the growth of my business and mapping out my programs just felt so natural. I was totally in the flow, enjoying every single second of growing my business. I'd wake up each morning at 5am, sometimes even earlier to pour everything into my company. I'd then go to work and return fourteen hours later and get straight back into it. It wasn't out of fear that I worked but out of love, out of passion.

Fear would have been working from a place of panic or desperation. Fear would have been working from a place of "I need to make the money ASAP so I can leave my job" Fear would have been procrastinating on things and holding myself back. Fear would have meant not investing in myself or getting the support I needed.

I remember when I was about to make my first big business investment by hiring a coach. It was more money than I ever imagined. It was definitely more money than I had available. Whilst many entrepreneurs have lots of fears and worries about whether their business will succeed and whether it would make money, I was directing my attention to being of service. My focus was creating, getting visible, sharing my message and showing up in the most authentic way that I could, driven by my love for helping others. As a result, the success and wealth seemed to flow into my life with relative ease. Clients came without me feeling like I was trying to find them. In fact, I had my first client request before I'd even got a proper website up.

That's the kind of amazing momentum you can create when you act from a place of love over fear. With my actions based out of love, I then strengthened my beliefs about myself and what I was worthy and capable of. I began to feel unstoppable. I believed I was worthy of huge amounts of success and abundance and so I began to witness success and abundance flooding into my life. I chose love and I manifested magic. As the saying goes "love always wins."

So how do we act from a place of love over fear? For me, this all really starts with the ability to love ourselves, something I've admittedly struggled with in the past. I remember really clearly a time when I was at school and it was an "own clothes" day. One of the girls from my friendship group came in and looked amazing. She'd curled her hair into these amazing waves, had her eyelashes and eyebrows tinted, had got nail extensions with a french manicure and had gotten a spray tan. In the eyes of a fourteen year old girl, this was the equivalent of Extreme Makeover. She was also wearing Some Miss Sixty bootcut jeans and this really cool halter neck top. It was the early Noughties, so you get the idea! In my insecure, fourteen-year-old, skinny body which hadn't yet developed, the teenage acne that had just started to sprout and my lank hair which looked greasy no matter how often I washed it, I felt the twang of jealousy as I saw my friend walk into class.

"Her hair looks like a poodle!" I remember saying to another of our friends who laughed with me. "What is she wearing?"

We didn't actually say any of this to the girl's face, but it was still a horrible thing to say and I remember how awful I felt as soon as the words left my mouth. They didn't make me feel good. For days, I beat myself up for saying something so mean. I wasn't a mean girl, but I did have mean thoughts about myself which I was then projecting onto others.

This is the thing about Self Love, if we don't possess enough of it, it turns us into people we are not. We may say or do mean things, we may get angry or resentful, we may block people out of our lives completely. We act out of fear rather than love. To act from a place of love, we first need to love and honour ourselves. The most important relationship we have should be with ourselves. We are our first, last and forever kind of love.

To cultivate true Self Love, you have to allow yourself to be led by your desires rather than being dictated by what you fear. True Self Love is about honouring your core passions and values and allowing yourself to show up as the most authentic version of you, making choices that truly light you up and being unapologetic about it. True Self Love means dropping any expectations about what you should do from family/teachers/society and trusting your own intuition to guide you.

The fourteen-year-old me didn't know much about Self Love. It's not something they really teach you in school. Whilst my parents did their best to raise me as a confident and independent young lady, they didn't know how to teach me how to program my thoughts, master my mind or connect with my higher self. They don't even know how to do this themselves. It's not something we are ever really taught from traditional schooling.

We learn things like maths and science and history, but crazily enough, at school, we aren't given any sort of lessons about how to transform our mindset or manage our emotions or overcome our fears. I'm sure if we were, the world would be a far better place. Instead, for many of us, school actually invokes more fear in us than it does love. It teaches us far more about taking action from fear than it does from love.

A lot of what we do in school is to tick boxes and jump through hoops. We are taught to conform, rather than being given the freedom to explore what really lights us up. Teachers put pressure on us to get good grades, not always out of love, but out of fear of maintaining school standards. Often we study not because of a burning passion for the subject, but because we are afraid of failing. Or, in the opposite case, we fear we will fail and therefore don't even try.

Now when I say that my teenage years were driven by fear over love, this isn't to say I wasn't raised by a loving family or those who had good intentions for me. What I mean, is that I think that society as a whole often operates from a place of fear by default. We don't know any different. We think we are doing the best we can, but if we open ourselves up to love a little more, things may look a little different.

Take, for example, my parents. I was the first person in my whole family to go to University. Now there is no denying that this was my choice. I wasn't pushed to go and was incredibly excited to study Law in London, however, my parents and teachers were definitely an influencing factor. I remember one Parents Evening when I told my parents and my English teacher that I loved writing and so wanted to be a journalist.

My teacher's reaction was to tell me she wouldn't want that for me as she feared it would make me into a horrible person. She explained that it's "dog eat dog" in the journalist world. That one, fear based comment altered my entire career path. After that evening, I cemented my decision to study Law over English Literature. Any sort of vision I had for writing was halted in its tracks.

My parents then encouraged my decision to study Law. My mum was bouncing off the walls with excitement about the thought of me becoming a lawyer, given that no one in our family had ever even been to university. While she had all good intentions and wanted the best for me, I know now that nudging me in this direction was her own fear-based response. This type of career was a "safe" option. It provided security and the promise of being financially stable, which I'm sure is what any loving parent wants for their offspring.

Rather than asking me what I really wanted, rather than anyone saying to me "what is the thing that brings you incredible amounts of joy?", I was never really given the option to pursue any alternatives. I didn't even question my decision, despite the fact that deep down, I probably knew that I wasn't being true to me. I knew deep down I was creative. I was not meant to wear a grey suit and sit under fluorescent office lights in an itchy swivel chair. I wasn't meant to tediously amend contracts or read through reports or attend weekly meetings on matters I had no real passion for.

I loved being surrounded by beauty, by nature, I loved the feeling of being free and travelling. I loved to write and to read and to design and to create. I loved to daydream up ideas. I loved to plot and plan creative ventures. For a while, I thought my entrepreneurial spirit developed later on in life but looking back now, I think it was there all along.

My parents, teachers and myself had all chosen fear over love. The result was, I ended up some place far removed from what I truly desired. If I'd have been taught the principles of true Self Love; how to transform my beliefs, how to strengthen my mindset and self-worth, how to conquer my fears, how to love every inch of myself unconditionally and how to trust my own intuition, my younger years may have looked a lot different.

Having said that, I believe we discover things at exactly the moment we are meant to and hidden in my past are countless lessons that have helped me become the person I am today. While there are a lot of decisions I regret making, I know that these have all led me to where I am now. The exact same can be said for you and your beliefs right now.

While you may have identified the beliefs that have so far kept you playing small or held you back, those same beliefs have led you to this moment and even if you are not where you want to be right now, know that moving forwards you have the power to change your beliefs and your reality.

I would like to finish this chapter with another exercise. It's an exercise that will help you to be more kinder with yourself and to start reframing what you believe about yourself. It's an exercise that I love inviting my clients to do and I'm sure you will get a lot of benefit from this too.

The Letter of Self Compassion Exercise

We are often our own worst enemies when it comes to our own internal dialect, yet when it comes to addressing others, we can show compassion with ease. Think about the last time someone came to you with a problem, something that they were struggling with or failed at and they were blaming themselves for it. Did you respond to them with compassion?

So let's say for example a friend comes to you and she tells you that she's been eating terribly, not exercising and feels really awful about herself and how she's looking. How would you respond? Would you say "yes you're so lazy and it's disgusting how you stuff your face with junk food?" Or would you be compassionate and speak with kindness, offering some constructive advice.

Chances are you'd do the latter. But think about what you'd say to yourself in the same situation because many of us wouldn't speak to ourselves with the same level of kindness. I had a client who was a part of our coach certification program. She had decided to book in with me for a 1:1 session as she was struggling with her own fears and limiting beliefs.

One of the first things she began telling me about was how she'd been doing some practice coaching with a client who'd been finding herself self-sabotaging because her inner voice kept telling her that she was "not good enough" to become a success in business. I asked my client how she responded, and I watched as her face lit up as she told me how she'd supported her through these fears.

For her own client, she could respond with love and compassion. She was able to offer her words of wisdom with kindness. But when it came to overcoming her own inner demons, she couldn't break the negative self-talk.

Sometimes we can be incredible cheerleaders for others, yet struggle when it comes to giving ourselves the same kind of treatment. This exercise can help with this.

Start by thinking about something you often beat yourself up about. It may be something you don't like about yourself, something that you feel inadequate at or something you've failed at. Think about how this makes you feel. Angry? Sad? Frustrated? Insecure?

Next, I want you to write a letter to your best friend, sharing everything that has come up for you. Get all of your emotions off your chest, letting your friend know exactly what you're struggling with internally right now and how it's making you feel.

Next, I want you to read the letter back and imagine you have just received this from a friend. How does this make you feel? I want you to write a response as if you are writing back to this friend to give them love, support and compassion. What would you say to soothe your friend?

Then, read back that letter. Read it to yourself, knowing that these are the words you need to read right now. Keep this letter with you and every time you find your inner critic creeping in, read the letter back to yourself.

Doing this is a powerful way to stop that inner mean girl in her tracks and turn beliefs of "you're not good enough" into something more loving and compassionate.

Raise Your Vibration

When your vibration is a match to your desire, all things in your experience will gravitate to meet that match every time. ~ Abraham Hicks

Everything on this planet is made up of energy. You are energy. Money is energy. Love is an energy. The thoughts you think are energy. While the Law of Attraction dictates that like attracts like, and The Law of Vibration dictates that everything vibrates at a certain energy, The Law of Transmutation states that you can trigger positive changes in your vibration.

Pack these all together, and you will realise that your vibration (your energy) dictates what you attract into your reality. You are a magnet to the things which you are a vibrational match to, and if you want to attract more positive experiences, you need to transform your energy so that you vibrate at a higher frequency.

Transforming yourself at an energetic level then is the next step in the process to manifesting the life you deserve and is intrinsically linked with Self Love. As you start to truly love yourself and start to feel better about yourself, you raise your vibration. Then, as you raise your vibration, you become a magnet to miracles. When you change your energy, everything changes.

If you are attracting things that you do not desire, such as debt, bad relationships, poor health or a lack of success, you can change that by changing your energy. By letting go of negative energy and by raising your vibration, you can draw into your life more positive experiences.

Ever had one of those days where you just feel like crap? You wake up feeling groggy and tired and just a little bit grumpy. Well, I've had a lot of those days in the past and funnily enough, these days tend to go from bad to worse.

Our energy starting our day impacts our energy for the rest of our day and subsequently what we experience. Things go from bad to worse. But when you start your day feeling high-vibe and feeling like you can take on the world, the better it gets, the better it gets.

Our energy and how we show up in the world affects everything. It can alter the types of friends we attract, the romantic relationships we manifest, the kinds of opportunities made available to us, our career or business success and also our wealth.

Manifesting money is an area that I'm hugely passionate about helping women transform, mainly as it has been an area of my life that has been completely overhauled. A lot of my own clients come to me because they are struggling to create wealth and know that it's something to do with their mindset or their energy that is holding them back.

I want to quickly share with you a story about one of our clients for whom changing her energy had a huge impact on the money she was able to bring into her business. In one of our coaching programs, The Clique Elite, we teach our clients how to scale their coaching business and an important part of this is sales. We teach our clients how to sell their premium coaching programs which they price at anything from £2000 to £10,000 The sales part of the business is something that a lot of our clients struggle with. In fact, I think a lot of women in general struggle with conversations around money and asking for money and charging their worth.

What a lot of our clients don't realise though is that when it comes to sales, 10% is what you say and 90% is how you show up into the call and your own vibrational frequency. One client, in particular, had spent a whole week taking calls from potential clients only to hear no after "no" after "no." The more "no's" she heard, the more disheartened she became.

Her vibration got progressively lower to the point where even the parts of her business which were previously working, also started to grind to a halt or present her with issues. One day, her website just crashed for no apparent reason, and the following day, some content she had been working on seemed to vanish from her computer.

While some people may put this down to bad luck or blame it on having "just one of those weeks", I knew it was all about her energy. I told my client to spend a week purely focusing on her, her vibration, her energy, and doing what she could to make herself feel great again. I encouraged her to start shifting her attention away from what was going wrong and instead focusing on other things in her life which were going well.

In situations where things just seem to be going from bad to worse, it's easy to dwell on the things that aren't working out, but remember that what you focus on expands. The more you pay attention to the things in your life which aren't working out, the more things won't work out. When you move your thoughts over to things that make you happy and grateful and positive, the more you attract positive experiences into your life. Thinking positive raises your energetic frequency and you therefore become a magnet to more high vibe things. In my clients case, these high vibe things were clients, sales and money in the bank.

A week after purely focusing on her energy without doing anything more, my client reported back to me that she was feeling incredibly positive about her business. While she wasn't really taking much action, she felt that something big was coming her way.

Now here comes the magic. A few days later, I had an email from my client to tell me that she'd just signed up someone into her program who had paid in full. I was so happy for her but had a feeling this was just the start of things. I was right. A week later the client sent me an email saying she wanted to jump on a quick call with me as she had some news. My gut told me that I was about to be celebrating a major milestone with her and sure enough, when we hopped on the call, she was bursting with excitement.

She explained to me that she had just had her biggest income week to date and made over ten thousand pounds over just seven days. She hadn't changed anything in terms of her product, her marketing or what she was saying on her calls. The only thing she had changed in her business was her own energy.

It's not just money that your energy impacts. I've had clients who have spent years dating ass hole after ass hole hoping that if they kiss enough frogs, eventually The One will appear. Just by shifting their energy and raising their vibration, their dream guy shows up seemingly out of nowhere and shakes up their world for the better. I've heard from women that have received promotions at work, not from "working harder" or doing more, but from transforming their energy.

Energy work is powerful, but what do I mean by changing your energy and raising your vibration, and what can you do to make the shift? Well let's just start with what you are giving your attention to.

I want you to take a moment and think about something that makes you feel anxious or scared or sad. Pick a specific thing, person or event. Sit with that thought for a few minutes and start to notice what is going on with your emotions. What kind of reaction are you experiencing in your body?

We can use our emotions as a guide to tell us what our energy is doing and whether we are high vibe or low vibe and whether we are inviting more of the things we want into our life, or more of the things we don't want. Our thoughts create how we feel, and when we think negative thoughts, we tend to not feel great.

As a result, our vibration is lowered, and we experience more negative experiences. Like attracts like. But if we allow thoughts into our minds thoughts that make us feel happy, confident, wealthy, successful, we will attract people, opportunities and things into our lives that make us feel even more happy, confident, wealthy and successful. Like attracts like.

So it's important then that we focus more on what we want rather than on what we don't want. Think positive thoughts, feel positive emotions, create more positive energy and then receive more positive experiences. Like attracts like.

Your energy is all about how you feel. You attract based upon your beliefs, but also how you feel, which is why for a lot of people, affirmations or vision boards just don't work for them. They say the words or look at the pictures without really feeling the feelings of what it would be like to be that person or to have those things. You can't just say "I am wealthy" over and over again without any sort of emotion attached to it and expect it to change your life. It's the energy behind the words that are important. Your energy needs to match what you want to create. So, if it's wealth you want to manifest, you need to be vibrating at the energy of wealth.

But what does that even mean?! I hear you ask. Well, this is where "Acting As If" comes into play which is one of my favourite tools for helping you feel incredible and also for manifesting some pretty incredible things into your life.

Act As If You Already Are Where You Want To Be - Jack Canfield.

"Acting as if" basically means thinking and acting in alignment with the version of you who already has everything you desire. Ever hear of the expression "dress for the job you want, not the job you have?" Well, it's the same kind of thing. If we show up thinking and acting like we are already bossing it in life, that we already are in the perfect relationship, that we already have the money in the bank, that we already are the super successful entrepreneur or high flying career woman, then we will start to attract and manifest as if this were true.

The more we start to act and think as the higher version of us would, the more we feel as if we already are that person. It's almost like the idea of "fake it until you make it', which was a philosophy I used to live by when I was just starting out in my business and was really struggling with my confidence as an entrepreneur. I decided that a good way to get myself out there and to help people find out about my coaching was through guest speaking or creating live content.

Let me just start by saying that I was petrified of any sort of live public speaking. It could be at an in-person event or going live online, I would feel physically sick at the thought of it. I remember the first time I went live online. It was before the times of Facebook Live when a platform called Periscope was just taking off. It was a platform that allowed you to live stream videos and anyone who wanted to could tune in. I had made a commitment to myself that I wanted to start sharing value with people and being a source of inspiration and decided that I would use Periscope to start live streaming.

The day I decided to go live, I had what I wanted to say planned and had rehearsed a gazillion times in the mirror before pressing the button on my phone to start the live streaming. After a few minutes of waffling on, I completely lost my train of thought and went into a mild panic. I was the victim of total word vomit where nothing that came out of my mouth was really making any sense. Rather than take a few moments to collect my thoughts and just breathe, I dramatically launched my phone across the room, sending it skidding across the floor.

Now, I'm sure the three "fans" that were watching at the time didn't really care, but I offered the explanation of technical difficulties and vowed to myself to never go live again. However, when you have a huge vision for your business and the impact you want to have on the world, putting yourself out there and sharing your message becomes a non-negotiable.

I knew if I wanted to make a significant impact with my work, I would need to get visible and share my knowledge so that people realised I existed. Live streaming or public speaking was a powerful way to do this. I knew I'd need to overcome this fear I had. My solution was to "fake it until I made it."

I started to think about how the super successful, influential coach who already had thousands and thousands of followers would think and act and I decided to embody the version of me that had already created what I wanted to achieve. I realised that the higher version of me didn't get herself flustered about the thoughts of speaking to an audience, but instead owned the stage and shared her message in an authentic and captivating way.

I realised that the woman who already had all I desired didn't slum it in yoga pants all day, but wore clothes that made her feel wealthy and successful. The woman I wanted to be had no time for Netflix binges or catching up on celeb gossip on the Daily Mail Online and instead, chose to fill her time and mind with things that served her bigger purpose and mission.

I started to write down each night in my journal about the woman I wanted to become and then went to sleep thinking as if I already was her and what that life would be like. I would think about how I would show up, what choices I would make, how I would speak and what I would say and then, as I went about my daily life, I would start to act as if I was that woman as much as I could. I started to align my thoughts and actions with someone who already possessed what I wanted to possess.

I later read a book by fashion designer Diane Von Furstenberg, and as it turned out, this was a strategy she had used too to help her become the woman she needed to be to get her to where she wanted to go. Well, if it's good enough for DVF, it's good enough for me, and it's good enough for you too.

I want you to start thinking about what you want your life to look like but more specifically, the woman you will be when you get there. Take some time with your journal and start to write out how the higher version of you who already has the relationship/money/success/happiness/confidence would show up. How does she dress? What does she think? How does she talk? How does she interact with others? How does she react to situations?

What is really interesting is that the more you start to align yourself with this person, the more you will start to manifest the people, things, opportunities, success and wealth that you would imagine this person to possess. You will find that things start showing up in your life that match the vision you have for your future and your future self.

So let's just take my situation as an example. As a new entrepreneur live streaming for the first time, I was not acting as if I already had the success I wanted to create. There I was, flapping around like a total amateur, unsure of myself, lacking confidence in my abilities, throwing phones across the floor. Was this how my highest version of me who already had everything I desired acted? I think not.

I needed to step up my game, so I started to not only read through my written description of the version I wanted to be every night, but I would also start to act as if I was cast as the leading lady in the story of my life. I acted like I was "playing the part". While deep down, I may not have had huge amounts of confidence in myself and my abilities as a coach, I would start to show up as if I did.

One example of this was when I agreed to be one of the main speakers at an event being held in London. It wasn't a huge audience at around fifty women, but it was certainly out of my comfort zone. Previously, taking part in anything like this would have made me feel physically sick but now, I had an tool I could put to use - Acting As If.

In the run up to the event, I got super intentional about how the higher version of me would show up. I wrote a detailed description of the event as if it had already happened and spoke of how confident and eloquent I was as I delivered my message. I also played out how the whole event was going to go in my mind first. I thought about what I'd wear, how I'd feel, what I'd say to the other women in attendance, the speech itself, the audience hanging on my every word, the round of applause after I finished and how proud I'd feel of myself once it was over. I imagined women coming up to me, telling me how much they loved my talk and how inspired they were by me.

Thinking about something you want to excel in before it actually happens is exactly how a lot of pro sports people achieve their results. The golfer will see herself hit the ball into the hole on the first swing. The tennis player sees herself serving a winning serve. If you can see it in your mind first, you can create it in your reality. By embodying the version of you within your mind first, you align yourself with the vibration of already having your desired outcome.

As it turned out, the event was a huge success. I not only felt like a total Girlboss after delivering my speech, but the impact of the event had a profound impact on my business. I began to get emails inquiring to work with me, I started to get introduced to other successful entrepreneurs, and my audience began to grow. I acted as if I'd already created the success I wanted and soon enough started to attract it. Like attracts like. The more I embodied the higher version of me I wanted to become who already had all of my desires, the more I became that woman and the more I attracted my desires into my life.

If you want something, you have to act as if you already have it and in doing so, you align your energy with your desires. When your energy matches what you want to attract, soon enough, your desires will be yours.

One question my clients ask in relation to this is "how can you act as if you are rich if you are broke," so let me just explain what I mean here because I don't want you to think acting as if you are wealthy means going crazy at the Chanel store. Whilst we have to trust that there is an abundance of wealth available to us and that when we spend money, it will come back to us tenfold, we also have to act financially responsible. We have to weigh up what is possible for us right now and prioritise our spending in a way that is in line with our higher vision. It doesn't mean you have to be tight with your money and not spend money that is available or save it all for a rainy day. Instead, it means you are able to spend money easily and freely, but not to the extent that you feel guilty for your purchase afterwards.

Remember, the whole point of "Acting As If" is to make you feel good. The idea is to transform your energy and raise your vibration so that you become a vibrational match to your desires. If you spend beyond your means to the point that afterwards, you become riddled with guilt, that kind of energy won't serve you.

The way I look at spending is by asking myself "how would this purchase help me get closer to the version of me who already has everything I desire." To begin with, this meant that rather than spending my money on designer handbags or luxury travel, I would ask myself "how could I use this money to help myself or my business grow?" To this day, most of my money is reinvested back into my business or spent on personal development as these are the things that are taking me closer to my ultimate destination.

Very rarely have I spent money on my own personal or spiritual growth or the growth of my business and regretted the decision and more often than not, my choices have helped me make far more money in the long run. In fact, whatever I spend in a way that is in alignment with my higher vision, The Universe always rewards me with far more in return. When you take a leap of faith towards the woman you know you are meant to be and the life you are meant to love, The Universe will always be there to support you.

I'd also like to point out that acting as if you're wealthy doesn't always mean spending crazy money. There are certain things you can do right now to feel as if you are already wealthy without needing to break the bank. You can wear something that makes you feel incredible. You can go and get a mani-pedi or buy yourself fresh flowers. You can have a really decadent bubble bath with some luxury bath oils, scented candles and pour yourself a glass of Prosecco and pretend it's the finest champagne.

One thing I also loved to do quite frequently was to "road test" my dream life. What I mean by this is I would spend an hour or sometimes even a full day acting as if I was already living how I wanted to live. I would drive past my dream house, imagining myself getting out of the car, walking up the driveway, through the front door and into the beautiful hallway with huge lofty ceilings and beautiful oak floors. I'd go into high-end stores and try on beautiful clothes or shoes, pretending in my mind that I had been invited to these incredible events where I'd be networking with other successful entrepreneurs.

In fact, one day, Philip and I did go out and actually road test a car we both really loved. Just twelve months after doing this, I was able to buy the exact same model in cash. I felt as if I already had it and soon enough, I actually did.

This has happened in so many areas of my life that I can no longer put it down to coincidence or luck. This is evidence of The Universe working its magic.

One area of your life you could upgrade without it needing to cost the earth is your environment. Your environment can have a huge impact on your vibration. Think about it: how do you feel when you walk into a beautiful space such as a spa? You feel amazing, right? The energy of the room has an impact on your own vibration.

When I started my business, I didn't have a beautiful office space that made me feel like a successful entrepreneur so one of the other ways I'd raise my vibration would go and take myself and my laptop to one of London's five-star hotels, order a coffee and work. I'd imagine that I was there on a business trip and was staying at the hotel. The beautiful surroundings would help me feel like I already was the successful and abundant business owner. For a while, I would completely forget that tomorrow I was back to my soul-destroying job, hustling to build my business on the side and slumming it in a flat that certainly wasn't luxury.

I was able to raise my vibration and feel successful and wealthy all for the price of a cup of coffee. Sure, you may not be able to afford to stay at a luxury hotel, but it costs very little to go and hang out there for the day.

Imagine living in a space that only contains things that spark joy ~ Marie Kondo

While we are on the topic of the impact of our environment on our energy, I want to share something that is going to revolutionise your life. It sounds like a bit of a boring suggestion but the impact of doing it is phenomenal. Tidy up. Yep, clear out the junk, spring clean, get yourself organised. I promise it will be a total game-changer for the energy in your house. Remember how I said that everything is energy? Well this includes your surroundings.

Have you ever been into a room or a house and for something to feel a little off? You can't quite put your finger on it, but it just gives you a weird vibe. That's energy. Or, think about when you are somewhere beautiful. Imagine you are in a luxurious, tranquil spa. As soon as you step in, you feel calm, relaxed. That's energy.

Our environments have a huge impact on our own vibrational frequency, and if we want to feel amazing and therefore become a magnet for more amazing things in our life, it's important we pay attention to our surroundings.

When I first started my business, as I have already mentioned, myself and Philip were living together in the living room of a flat we shared with far too many housemates. Neither of us are minimalists. We both brought with us to our new shared living space a crazy amount of "stuff", the sole purpose of which was to clutter up the place. Philip decided that having five different types of sporting equipment (a cricket bat, a hockey stick, golf clubs, tennis rackets and a rounders bat) was totally necessary, despite him not playing any of these sports since he was sixteen.

I was no better, having carted with me a boatload of clothes from my "shopping like a maniac" years, many of which still had the tags on having never actually been worn. Keep in mind that we were living in a living room, a room which was never intended to be used as a bedroom and therefore we had zero storage. No wardrobe, no cupboards or drawers, nor any space to add in these essential pieces of furniture, meaning that our stuff was basically just collecting dust in piles on the floor.

At the time, I had started building my business on the side and was working mostly from my bed with my laptop strategically placed on a pillow which served as a makeshift desk. Needless to say, it wasn't the high vibe environment of the successful, abundant, influential entrepreneur I was striving to be.

When I started to learn about the importance of energy and the impact of your surroundings on your vibration, I began to question whether my living situation was really serving me. Thinking about it, I realised that working from bed wasn't exactly making me feel high vibe. In fact, whenever I would be on a client call, I almost felt a bit of a fraud trying to inspire them and empower them while I myself was slumming it behind the scenes.

I remember being on a sales call with a potential client, and when it came to the part of the call where I would share my prices, I froze. I just couldn't seem to get my words out. I almost felt like something was blocking me.

Needless to say, the client didn't sign up, despite it being someone I knew deep down I'd be able to help immensely. Now I realise that this again was energy at play. Vibrationally, I wasn't where I needed to be, and my surroundings were having a big impact on this. My low vibe living situation was causing me to attract low vibe experiences.

The next day, I set to work on creating a small space in the corner of my room from which I could work. I got myself a small desk and chair and bought some fresh flowers and a beautiful scented candle. By the flowers, I placed a few of my favourite crystals - a piece of Rose Quartz and a chunk of Citrine. Behind the desk was my vision board, mapping out all I was in the process of manifesting.

I then set to work, clearing out all of the things that didn't serve me. I got rid of bags of clothes that I didn't love. I threw away things I'd collected that I had zero attachment too but was holding onto them "just in case". I cleared away folders full of old receipts and paperwork. I basically "Marie Kondo'd" my life (which if you've not read Marie Kondo, "The Life-Changing Magic of Tidying" I urge you to go and grab yourself a copy ASAP)

The results were phenomenal. I instantly feel lighter. I had so much more clarity on my life, my business and my goals. I felt more positive about things and more confident in my approach. I began to feel more like the successful, abundant entrepreneur I wanted to be.

Clearing out and decluttering the space you live in is not just about getting organised. It's about shifting out stale energy that has been lingering and opening up space for you to receive new, amazing things into your life. Think about it. When you are somewhere that is clean and tidy, how much "lighter" do you feel? How much more energised do you feel? How much more clarity do you have on what you are doing and where you want to go? By getting rid of the things that didn't serve me at the highest level, I'd cleared the pathways for more clients, more success, more wealth, more exciting opportunities and better relationships.

While totally overhauling your home is a bit of a mammoth task, one thing you can start with is clearing out the room where you spend the most of your time and also the place where you keep your money, so your handbag and wallet.

One of my favourite areas I like supporting my clients with is manifesting is money. Money, like everything on this planet, is also just energy. Your ability to receive money is dependent on you being a vibrational match to the energy of money and wealth. You also need to have space to energetically receive money. I'd like you to think about where you currently keep your money and what kind of energy this is emitting.

Are your handbag and wallet stuffed full of old receipts, used train tickets, sweet wrappers, loose change or any other sorts of rubbish? Think about what kind of message this clutter is sending out to The Universe. It's basically sending out the energy of "I don't really care about my money, and, If you don't care about where you keep your money, The Universe isn't going to be in a rush to send you more.

Would you purchase a pair of beautiful designer shoes only to throw them into the bottom of a dirty cupboard? No, you would love and respect them by keeping them clean and neat in their box inside your wardrobe. The same needs to apply to your money.

How do you think it makes you feel if every time you reach into your handbag or wallet to pay for something and you are faced with a crazy mess, having to rummage through the junk in order to get to your money? This clutter can impact how you feel around money and how we feel around money affects our ability to manifest more money into our life. Having an organised place where you keep your money helps send out a message to The Universe that you respect money and can handle more of it.

Clearing out the junk also helps to energetically make space for money to physically enter your life. It's a simple thing you can do right now but it can actually have a huge impact on your own money frequency. To enjoy money manifesting into your life with ease, you have to have empowering experiences with money and simply getting organised with where you keep your money rather than rummaging through a sea of mess is a great place to start.

Another little tip is to keep crisp notes inside your wallet so that each time you look into your wallet, you are not presented with a barren waste land. Remember; we manifest based on how we feel, so when it comes to manifesting wealth, you have to do what you can to make yourself "feel wealthy", even if you aren't yet experiencing it in your physical world.

When you forgive you heal and when you let go, you grow.

As well as physically decluttering your life, chances are you also need to go through a bit of emotional decluttering too. When we hold onto negative emotions from past experiences, we can actually block positive manifestations from entering into our life.

Like attracts like meaning that we attract into our life things which we are a vibrational match to. Negative emotions equal to negative energy which lead to negative manifestations. So let's say you are holding onto fear and resentment. Chances are you will experience things in your physical world that will cause you to feel more fear and resentment.

I want you to think of your energy in its purest form as a bright white ball of light surrounding you. In this purest form, The Universe is easily able to send you it's gifts. Then imagine what happens when you are holding onto negative energy in the form of bad memories, emotional trauma, jealousy, fear, resentment or any other type of negative emotion. Think of this negative energy as black smudges splattering your pure white energetic field. These dark smudges absorb negative experiences and things but repel positive experiences and things from entering into your life. In order to cleanse your energy of these dark smudges, you need to let go of the negative energy you are holding onto. One of my favourite rituals for letting go of and releasing negative energy is forgiveness.

I think no matter who you are or what kind of life you've had to date, we can all benefit from forgiveness, whether it's forgiving ourselves, others or, more than likely, both. Forgiveness is a way to declutter your own energy and let go of negative emotions you may be holding onto because of the actions of yourself, or something that someone else has done.

To give you an idea of how this works in practice, I want to share my experience of using forgiveness in relation to my money story. Money and I, if you haven't guessed already, have had a pretty love/hate relationship. My answer to coping with the emotional pain caused by my relationship and my job was to spend money. I spent money like it was going out of fashion on anything and everything. I didn't respect money, and subsequently, money didn't stick around in my life for very long. All of the negative emotions I was feeling about myself and my low self-worth was causing me to repel positive experiences from coming into my life, money included.

How easily money is able to not only come into your life and stick around long enough for you to enjoy it but also pour back in as quickly as it is spent is all related to your self-worth. Transform how you feel about yourself and watch how much of a dramatic impact it can have on your bank balance.

Anyway, back to energy, and my own negative experiences I was holding onto when it came to my own finances. As my debts built up, I started to feel more and more ashamed about my spending. I'd not shared my debts with anyone, but it didn't still didn't stop me feeling terribly shit about the mess I'd gotten myself into. When I started my own healing process, I began to connect the dots between my poor financial choices and my self-worth and realised the extent to which I was using money as a way to make myself feel better, but long term it was actually doing more harm than good.

As I strengthened my self-worth and subsequently got a hold of my crazy spending, it didn't change the fact that I'd managed to accumulate over £20k worth of debt, debt that was causing me to feel massive amounts of shame and guilt. I was always getting angry with myself for letting things get so out of control. I would tell myself how stupid and irresponsible I had been. While I would claim to love money, talking about it wasn't something that made me feel good and so I, therefore, avoided all talks of it altogether. I wanted to manifest more of it into my life, but I simultaneously held all of these negative memories about money.

I like to think of these as abundance blocks. My prior negative money experiences were affecting my energy and causing me to subsequently block money from coming into my life. I was holding onto these fear and guilt and shame about money that I was repelling it. Every time money came in, it would find a way to disappear again very quickly. I had to, therefore, release these blocks of energy which were cluttering up my energetic field so I could open up the pathways for abundance to flow in.

The process which helped me with this was forgiveness. I had to forgive myself for how I had acted around money for money, and I had to forgive myself for allowing money to control me. I had to forgive myself for not getting on top of my finances sooner. I had to forgive myself for creating the financial mess I got myself into. It was only once I'd been through this forgiveness process that I could then start to witness money pouring into my life.

Forgiving yourself of how you have behaved in the past or choices you've made or things you've said or done is a way to release any negative energy you are holding onto and therefore clearing the way for more positive experiences to reach you.

It can also be used to help you release yourself from the impact others may have had on you. I not only used a forgiveness ritual for my money issues, but I also used the process to forgive the ex-fiancee. In doing so, I felt I was able to show up in my new relationship as a much more empowered, self-assured version of me. I forgave my ex for how he treated me. I forgave him for the pain he caused me and the anger I subsequently felt, and as I practised this forgiveness, I felt lighter. I let go of the negative memories and emotions and in doing so, invited the possibility for a new romance to appear in my life.

When I met my now partner Philip, I was able to put everything into that relationship. I was able to allow myself to be vulnerable. I was able to give love and receive it, and that relationship is now as solid as a diamond and has given me my beautiful daughter.

Forgiveness is your opportunity to heal yourself from unwanted memories or negative emotion so that you can let go and grow into the life you were made for. So how do we forgive ourselves or others? Whilst there are a number of rituals you can use, I love the Ho'oponopono prayer. The prayer is an ancient Hawaiian practice where you write out all of the things you need to forgive yourself of another before repeating the mantra "I'm sorry, please forgive me, thank you, I love you'. I like to then seal the ritual by burning the paper to signal the release.

Your Vibe Attracts your Tribe

Now, it's one thing to forgive people for who have negatively impacted our past, but what about people who are currently having a negative impact on our lives? While we can forgive them, how do we prevent them from undoing all the work we are putting into our own personal and spiritual development?

If you've ever heard the phrase, "your vibe attracts your tribe", you will understand that you are the product of the people you spend the most time with. Who you hang out with has a huge impact on your own vibrational frequency and therefore what you go on to manifest and the kind of life you live. If you are around people who are constantly complaining about life, always talking negatively about others and just generally being a bit of a Debbie Downer, it's hard to keep yourself positive. How often have you found yourself in a situation where you've found yourself contributing to a conversation that isn't particularly positive only to leave the conversation feeling a bit shit about yourself and life in general?

Or alternatively, have you ever found yourself in a room filled with positive, high energy, optimistic people? What kind of impact did that have on your own energy? As I stepped into the entrepreneurial world, I made it my mission to surround myself with high vibe women, women who were achieving amazing things, spreading positivity in the world, inspiring others and just generally keeping the vibe upbeat. This is so important.

Look at your current circle. Who have you got in your life that lifts you higher? If you visit www.daniwatson.com/selfloveclub and join the Self Love Club, you will be invited into our free Facebook community where you can network with like-minded women who are also on a mission to grow themselves personally, spiritually, financially and professionally. I suggest if you've not got a high vibe tribe yet, then get yourself into that group for a heavy dose of daily inspiration and women supporting each other.

For the people in your life who are negative, take yourself away from the conversation. Just don't engage in gossip or bitchiness or complaining. This isn't to say you can't be there for people when they really need you, but a lot of people just love to have a good moan about the same thing over and over again without actually doing anything about it, and they will drag you into the conversation. Misery loves company. Engaging in these kinds of conversations drains your own energy and rarely leaves you feeling good.

Change the topic by guiding the conversation onto something different or even better, bring them on this personal growth journey with you. If they aren't willing to do this, then it's their loss, and it shouldn't mean that you need to suffer.

Not everyone is going to "get it" when it comes to Law of Attraction, The Universe, mindset etc. and that's ok. You just do you and find others who will support you in this. I once had a friend email me with the subject line: "The meaning of crystals". She'd never really shown much interest in my work and had actually made a few sarcastic remarks about my connection with The Universe. She clearly wasn't into anything remotely spiritual or to do with mindset and even thought Yoga was a bit "woo woo" and that was fine.

When I saw her email come through, I thought how sweet it was of her to send it across to me, knowing that crystals were my thing. I opened up the email, but it wasn't what I expected. Instead, it was an image titled "The meaning of crystals" with images of different crystals underneath, but next to each picture where the meaning should be it said, "Crystal Meaning = Nothing, It's a rock!"

Now, thankfully, I'm not someone who takes things to heart too much and was able to see the funny side, but it just reminded me that not everyone will get it. You will have some friends that will obsess over Rose Quartz with you, tag along with you as you go to your gong bath and join you in your Ayahuasca ceremony. Then there will be others who will think it's all a load of hippy-dippy bullshit and that's ok too. Just don't let them derail you from your vision or your goals. Don't let others dictate your own personal growth.

If you're reading this book, it's because it's something you were meant to discover and I hope I've opened up your eyes to a world where you have no limits as to what you can achieve or who you can become. If others laugh, let them laugh. You keep doing you and keep walking your authentic path because when you do, The Universe will validate it.

Daring to set boundaries is about having the courage to love ourselves, even when we risk disappointing others - Brene Brown

While we are on the conversation of others and the impact other people can have on our vibration, let's talk about boundaries. Having proper boundaries in your life is so important in order to preserve your energy, honour your time and to protect you from the negative energies of others.

So often, we say "yes" to things because we feel like we are bound by duty when really, it doesn't serve our highest interests. Maybe it's saying "yes" to a social invite despite the fact you feel exhausted because you don't want to upset a friend.

Maybe it's saying "yes" to loaning someone money, despite not feeling comfortable with it. Maybe it's allowing someone to take up a lot of your time and energy, so much so that your own needs aren't being served.

We all have ways in which we allow our boundaries to be tested or pushed, but it's important that we preserve our boundaries so that we can show up in the world as the highest vibe version of ourselves. It's important to remember that you cannot serve from an empty cup. If you give everything you have to the needs and wants of others, you will get to a point where you have nothing left to give. You'll not only have nothing left to give to your own wants and needs, but you will also no longer have the capacity to give to loved ones. This is where boundaries become crucial.

We can give to others and give in abundance, but not to the extent that it depletes our own resources. Respecting our boundaries is often tied to the balance of duty versus desire. Too often we act out of duty, rather than desire, making choices based on what we feel we should do rather than what we really want to do and what we know is right for us.

One of my clients recently came to me so burned out by her sense of duty, that she no longer felt like she had anything left to give. She was torn between her duty to her business, her family and her friends to the point where her desires were being completely disregarded. She found herself with very little time for herself and her own desires because she was too caught up in saying yes to the needs and desires of others. This led her to experience complete burnout and overwhelm to the point that she was then no use to anyone.

Remember: Self Care isn't selfish. It's necessary. To practice true self-care and ultimately Self Love, we need to have in place proper boundaries that protect our energy and ensure we can shine our light in the brightest possible way. Setting boundaries is something I encourage all my clients to do to help them maintain a high vibration. Some examples of how you can protect your boundaries are as follows:

- Allowing yourself to say no to people or things that don't serve you WITHOUT feeling guilty.
- Managing your time effectively so that you actually pencil in time for your own self-care and commit to it as if it was an important business meeting. You should always make room in the day for something that is purely for you and you alone.
- If you're in a client-facing business, have rules in place for when and how clients can communicate with you so that your time is not taken advantage of by your clients.
- Be mindful of "over-delivering" with clients and finding yourself doing or offering more than what you initially agreed to.
- Maintain boundaries when it comes to your prices by being firm about what you charge

and not allowing potential customers/clients to test your boundaries by asking for discounts/freebies.

- Speak your mind when you feel someone has overstepped your boundaries, and it's left you feeling frustrated.

- Understand your own boundaries and limits on how much you work. It's important to know what your cut off point is and when inspired action begins to feel like forced action, and it's time for you to step away from your desk.

Gratitude is a magnet for miracles ~ Gabby Bernstein

No chapter on energy would be complete without a discussion on the importance of gratitude. When you change your energy to the energy of gratitude, you become a magnet for the most delicious and exciting experiences to manifest into your life. The quickest way to getting whatever you want in life is to be grateful for where you are at right now. This means being grateful for what you have, but also for who you are.

Remember the morning ritual I spoke of at the beginning of this book? Well gratitude through journaling is a part of this ritual, and if you practice gratitude as part of your morning routine, you will reap the rewards. When you practice gratitude, The

Universe presents you with more and more reasons to feel grateful..

Within this chapter are some Gratitude Journal Prompts you can use as part of your daily routine. Spend some time each morning writing our gratitude statements for the things in your life you are already grateful for, and you shift your energy into a place of abundance over lack.

This is so important. When we set ourselves goals or get clear on our desires, it's so easy to view these things from a place of lack. For example "I want the house that I don't yet have." Or "I want the relationship, but I'm currently single." Shifting your focus to the energy of gratitude helps you to focus on the presence of things, rather than the absence of things.

We all have something in our life right now for us to be grateful for. The fact you are breathing and alive and living in a world with so much potential is itself something to be celebrated. The fact you have found your way to this book is also something to be grateful for. Hopefully, you have at least one person in your life right now that fills your world with joy. We have sun. We have flowers. We have The Internet. Even if it feels like you've not a lot to be grateful for right now, if you look around you, the world is abundant with things to be grateful for.

Gratitude can be given for what you have, but also what you want to manifest. This relates back to

"Acting As If" and creating the feeling of already having what you desire. Don't just thank The Universe for what you already have, but thank The Universe for everything you want as if it is already yours. You can do this as part of your daily journaling practice.

Rather than writing down your goals and getting specific about what you want from a place of wanting these things to manifest, write them down from a place of already having these things through gratitude statements.

For example, "I'm so grateful for the amazing and successful business I have built." Or "I'm so grateful for the beautiful dream home I live in" While you write out these statements, create the energy of already having these things by imagining what it would feel like to have these things in your life right now. When you start to pay attention to the abundance that is already present through gratitude, you quickly allow the life you want to manifest right before you.

Gratitude Journaling Prompts

These journaling prompts can be used as part of your daily gratitude practice. You don't need to use them all at once. Simply pick a few each day.
What special someone has taught you about unconditional love in the past or present?

Write down one good thing that happened to you today.

What are five personality traits that you are most thankful for?

What about your upbringing are you most grateful for?

In what way are you happy with how your day turned out?

Name 5 things you are doing well currently.

Did you have a nice surprise today? Write about it.

Did you do something nice for someone today? Write about it.

What family members are you most grateful for? Write about what makes them special?

What friends are you most grateful for having? List what makes each friend special.

List something good that has recently caught your attention to make you realize how fortunate you are.

Think about the worst period you went through in your life and list 10 ways life is better now than it was then.

Declutter Your Living Space Exercise

Commit to clearing out the space in which you live from things that do not serve you. Where are you holding onto things that you do not use or do not love? Where are you keeping this "just in case", knowing deep down that they do fit in with the dream life you want to create?

Self Love is about allowing ourselves to let go of the things you know do not really serve you. Self Love is about clearing out old energy to make ready for the higher vibrational things that you deserve. Set aside some time to declutter and free up room for more amazing things to manifest into your life.

Inspired Action

Action that is inspired from aligned thoughts is joyful action ~ Abraham Hicks.

So far within this book, the conversation has been all about the mindset; your beliefs, your thoughts, how you feel and your energy. But let's remember that manifesting is about co-creating with The Universe. It's not about us asking for something, thinking positively and then what we want just falls from the sky into our laps. As nice as this would be, we have to show up and play our part. We have to take our steps and The Universe will meet us halfway.

This leads me onto the next part of the process, which is taking inspired action. You have to take action steps towards creating the life you want. You are not just a passive bystander in your life; you are the captain. You've not only got to let The Universe know what you want and do the inner work to shift your beliefs and energy, but you've also got to put the wheels into motion by doing things and putting yourself out there. A big part of Self Love is not just about how you feel about yourself, but having the confidence to act upon your desires and actually take the steps required to create a life that lights you up.

Let's say you want to manifest The One. Do you think you can just cocoon yourself in your bedroom and he's just going to show up on your doorstep one day? Of course not. You've got to be getting out and meeting people. Or, let's say you want to attract success within your business. You can't just sit thinking happy thoughts about clients and money and expect these things to appear. You have to be taking action.

One of the things I wanted more of in my life when starting my business was money. I was eventually able to begin manifesting much more of it, but it didn't just magically land in my bank account. I made it happen. I created my business, I put myself out there to promote myself online, I started creating content to build my audience, I began speaking at events, I hosted events. I created my programs, I built my team and I recorded videos for YouTube.

The money didn't just magically manifest. I created pathways for the money to show up. This is so important. What you do is just as important as what you think. Yes, you need to have powerful beliefs about yourself and what you are capable of, but these beliefs need to then be backed up by action. And not just any kind of action. It has to be inspired action.

Inspired action is action that feels good, action that brings you joy and that lights you up and comes from a place of ease and flow. You have to take action that keeps you in alignment. The whole point of working in your mindset, strengthening your self worth and raising your vibration is to get you into alignment. It helps you become a vibrational match to your desires.

There is no point in doing all of this inner work only to then do things that make you feel stressed, overwhelmed or just generally crappy. Sure, you can go sit on your meditation mat for an hour a day, but if you're then spending the rest of your time living in a way that doesn't make your heart sing, hustling hard and burning yourself out, it's going to undo all of that amazing progress you've made. Remember that we manifest based on how we feel so you've got to be able to take action that keeps your vibration high as much as possible. You've got to find the path of least resistance, a path that feels delicious and juicy for you, rather than going with what you think you should be doing or by doing the things that make you feel icky.

So let's say you are a business owner and you want to manifest more sales. You would love to have clients knocking at your door begging to work with you. You want to grow your business to become one of the best in the industry. If you're running your business in a way that is depleting you, zapping your joy, killing your mood and burning you out, it's going to take far longer to see success.

Believe me, because I've been there. There have been times in my business that I've been sucked into the hustle in a big way. I was all about "crushing goals" and "working today so my future self will thank me for it". I was hooked on the "go big or go home" mentality that a lot of entrepreneurs assume is the thing that will get them to the top.

Incidentally, this way of working didn't lead me anywhere fast. Every time I've found myself overworking, doing the things in my business that don't light me up and neglecting myself in the process, I've actually held myself even further away from my goals.

Burning ourselves out to get what we want needn't be the case. In fact, what if I was to tell you that manifesting what we want can happen far quicker when we work less rather than more, when we allow for things to be easy? Let me share a story with you that is evidence of this.

One of the biggest income leaps my company The Clique has ever had in one month was the month I'd actually worked less than I ever had done before. Each month, our team sits down, and we go through our numbers; how many new clients did we sign up, how much turnover did we make, how much profit did we make, how much of a percentage increase are we on from last month.

Typically we aim to go up around ten per cent each month, although some months this can be slightly more and some months, slightly less. This particular month, we actually doubled our sales. I fully believe because it was a month where I'd got myself fully into alignment and only made time for the thing that brought me joy. In fact, that month I'd spent a week out in Mykonos doing nothing more than eating delicious food, hanging out at beautiful beaches and generally having a great time. Most of my energy that month went into things that made me feel amazing.

Now, I should point out that I do have an incredible team to support me in my business and a marketing system that is largely automated which means my business model can allow me to take lots of time off, but this hasn't always been something I've found easy to do. In fact, one of the things I recognised in myself as a new business owner was that I was addicted to the struggle. I would gladly tell people about my early mornings and late nights as it made me feel important, like I was a busy woman running a busy empire.

And think about it; isn't that the exact picture society has painted of success? This idea that to be an influential, successful woman, we need to be working our butts into the ground? Think about films such as "The Devil Wears Prada", "I Don't Know How She Does It" or "The Holiday". These are some of my favourite films, yet interestingly, all of these films depict successful women who have had to make huge amounts of sacrifice or experience burnout in order to achieve their dreams. We are led to believe that this masculine type of energy is what is required of us for us to create the success that we want.

I'm not just talking about business or career success here either. I once had a client who was going on around five different dates a week (sometimes two dates in one day!) in order to find The One. She hated the process, was done with all the apps and ready to spend the rest of her life as some kind of modern-day Miss Havisham. She was not taking inspired action.

While she was taking big action, the action she was taking was making her feel crap about herself rather than feel better. We looked at what she could do to keep herself in action but in a way that served her. Rather than dating becoming this thing she "had to do", she decided to ditch the apps entirely and started to make more time for fun things she'd always wanted to try.

A month later, she met a guy at a kickboxing class (a class she'd always been wanting to try) they hit it off, and as far as I'm aware, they're still dating. We don't always need to do "more" to get what we want. We just need to do it in a way that feels fun and inspiring, in a way that excites us. True Self Love means inviting more joy into our lives, rather than opting for the difficult route.

This inspired action filters through a lot of the work I do with my clients. One of the programs we offer in The Clique is a business program which helps coaches scale their business online and in it, we encourage our clients to sit in their core zone of brilliance as much as possible. What we mean by this is that they should find the things they love doing and feel that they are meant to be doing as a business owner and double down on these activities, while outsourcing or delegating the bits that leave them feeling frustrated or overwhelmed.

This philosophy can also be applied outside of a business in that as we move through life, we should sit in our core zone of brilliance as much as we can. It may be dating in a way that feels exciting and brings out the best in you. It may mean choosing a diet or fitness regime that your body loves. It may mean doing work you are truly passionate about or making more time for the things you are really great at. Our core zone of brilliance is where the magic resides within us. Rather than suppressing this magic by sitting outside of our zone of brilliance, we should be igniting our magic by embracing our zone of brilliance as much as possible.

In order for us to fully live by this philosophy, it also means we need to start doing things for us and making choices that are true to us, who we are and what we really love rather than doing what we feel we ought to do or what is expected of us. Taking inspired action means to trailblaze our own authentic path towards our desires, doing things our way, without worrying about what others will say or what society conditions us to believe we should do.

Let's take manifesting a successful career, for example. Hands up how many of you reading this have chosen your career path based upon what you felt was expected of you either by parents, teachers, society or some other major influence in your life? And how many of you who have replied yes to the above question can truly say that you feel you've created the success you want and are 100% happy with how your career is developing?

I firmly believe that so many of us end up struggling to see the success we want because we are so attached to the picture of how we think it should be done, rather than going with what feels right for us. In fact, I think so many of us don't even know what true success means to us as we've been blinded by what we are shown in the media.

Success is portrayed to us as the flashy cars, the luxury travel, the mega mansions and sure, for some, this may be the ideal. But for many, it won't be. I've had clients who've told me coming into my programs that they want to become a millionaire business owner so that they can buy their dream home, only to share with me later than they now want to become a digital nomad and travel around the world in a campervan, spending most of their days surfing.

My point is, we are so easily influenced by the people and world around us that this can sometimes hold us back even further from what truly brings us joy. When it comes to taking action, I see so many women slipping into these ways of working/dating/exercising/making money, that just aren't serving them and they then wonder why things don't seem to be working out.

Another client of mine wanted to manifest, amongst other things, a better body. She'd always struggled with her weight, and no matter what exercise she tried or diet she attempted, nothing really seemed to work. Figuring out her "zone of brilliance" we realised that she loved going on walks and loved yoga, but she admitted that she'd never really stuck to doing these regularly as she didn't feel that they'd have a big impact.

Instead, she'd been trying high-intensity classes which she hated and became increasingly frustrated as they didn't really give her the results she hoped for. Alongside working on her self worth, her mindset and her vibration, she also committed to taking inspired action by doing the yoga and the morning walks that brought her so much joy. I'm sure you can guess what happened. As if by magic, her body started to change in a way that it never had before and she started to feel amazing in her own skin.

That's the beauty of taking inspired action. Not only does it help you get to your desired goal, but it allows you to enjoy the journey, and isn't that what it's all about anyway? We are not just here to get things done, to tick things off a list or to "arrive" at our destination. There has to be joy in co-creating. We have to do things that feel expansive and freeing and easy and fun.We have to do the things that lift us higher rather than dragging us down, otherwise what's the point? You will get to your goal and realise there is something "more" you want, and then you'll begin the process all over again, slogging away at things you simply don't enjoy doing just to get to your next milestone.

Now while we could all do with making room for more of what brings us joy, one of the things we could also all do a bit better at is how much action we are taking at any given moment. How often do you hear yourself saying how busy you are? People wear their busy-ness like a badge of honour. It's almost seen as a noble thing to be working hard. I remember when I worked in the city, it almost felt like it was a competition for who could stay at work the longest. People would boast about not leaving the office until 11 pm or working weekends. Busy has become our default way of living and guess what?! Busy doesn't always mean achieving more. How often have you gone about your day busy as a bee only to then get to then and wonder where exactly your time went and feeling like you don't really have anything to show for it?

What is interesting is that this attachment to being busy is often intrinsically linked to our sense of worth. We often believe that we are only worthy of success if we are earning our right to be successful through working hard. We struggle to believe that we deserve success simply for being ourselves. A low sense of worth then translates into "I need to do more/be more/work harder" to be worthy of succeeding.

Something that I discovered on my own mindset journey was that I didn't believe I was worthy of becoming a successful and abundant entrepreneur unless I was working incredibly hard all of the time. It's also a discovery that so many of my clients find out too. Because of my own lack of worth and a belief that I alone wasn't "enough", I felt like I needed to prove myself worthy of success. I felt like I had to "earn" my right to receive clients, money, opportunities, and support. I didn't believe I could have these things just for being me.

This need to prove my worth then translated into me doing more, working harder or generally being "busy". It's almost like deep down I had to first "suffer" before I would allow myself to receive. There have been times in my business and life that I've found myself falling into the "busy" trap and rarely has it got me to where I want to go.

One time, after a very "busy" period where I'd been working crazy hours putting together a new program, I found myself hitting a wall. I couldn't find the energy to create, to connect with my team, to conduct my coaching calls. In fact, being busy left me feeling uninspired to do anything at all. In an effort to prove myself and my worth, I'd overloaded myself to the point I'd zapped away any creativity whatsoever.

I was unable to show up as the best version of me for my business and my clients and I was certainly not "vibing high" What was interesting was the things I was keeping myself busy with were not my "zone of brilliance" things. In fact, most of what was keeping me busy were things outside of my zone of brilliance, things I didn't love, nor was I meant to be doing.

Here's the thing; there is a difference between being busy and being in the flow. Being busy rarely feels good. Being in the flow however, feels expansive. Think of it as being "in the zone", like when you feel so on fire and unstoppable that you feel you can take on the world. Being in the flow means you feel energised and empowered, not frazzled or burned out. Taking inspired action is the difference between being busy and being in the flow. If you want to manifest anything in life, you've got to take action but it has to be this delicious kind of juicy action that makes you feel on top of the world.

When you are busy for busy's sake, you risk putting yourself out of alignment with your desires. When we are busy for busy's sake, we are not loving ourselves as we should and not treating ourselves like the goddesses that we are.

Another interesting revelation I had when I started to identify the link between my worth and my need to work hard, was that my ability to work hard was always the thing I'd been praised for. At school, I was an A grade student. I love studying, and it was through my studies that I received a lot of my praise through my parents and teachers. Working hard was my way of being validated. It was how I received acceptance and, ultimately, love.

The reason why I'm sharing this with you, is because when I tried to break apart the link between my sense of worth and working hard, I struggled. I just couldn't seem to accept that I could achieve success without needing to try harder. I found it incredibly difficult to shake off the idea that action always needed to be an uphill struggle. No matter how much I wanted to believe that taking action towards my desires could be fun and light, I always found myself reverting back to the same patterns of overworking and overwhelm.

What I discovered was that not only was my sense of worth attached to how hard I was working, but it was the thing through which I derived my identity. If I wasn't working hard, who was I? My ability to work hard was something I'd always prided myself on and without it, what was left? Who would I be without my ability to work hard? What was I worth if not working hard? Healing these beliefs is something to this day that I still work on and if you resonate with this, one thing I'd suggest repeating is the following mantra:

I am enough. I do not need to do more or work harder. I am enough and I am able to receive all of my desires just by being me. I am enough.

One of my favourite Law of Attraction gurus is Esther Hicks, who channels The Universe through a non-physical collective of beings known as Abraham. One of the things she often says is that we have to take the path of least resistance, meaning that to manifest our desires, we have to allow things to be easy. We have to expect our desires to come easily. So how do we do this? Well, my first suggestion would be to brainstorm some of the action steps you could start doing right now that will lead you towards your goals and ask yourself which things light you up the most. Which of those things would you find the most joy doing? Then, start doing more of that. It's that simple.

Another thing you can do is to stop talking about how busy and difficult life is. The more you give attention to something, the more it becomes our truth. How many times has someone asked you how you are, and you've replied "busy! Your words have so much power. Every word you speak has energy behind it, energy that you are putting out into The Universe and The Universe then matches like with like and gives you more of what you're putting out. Talking about being busy leads to a busier and busier life. Instead, why not try switching tour words for something more empowering.

For example: "How are you today?" "Oh I feel amazing. So relaxed! So much time on my hands for me and doing the things I love." Next time someone asks you how you are, repeat back how you want to feel, rather than how busy or tired you are and see how much lighter and expansive that feels.

You also have to carve out free time as you would a business meeting. Making space for your own self-care is not selfish. It's crucial for keeping your vibe high and therefore attracting more good stuff into your life. Not only that but you cannot pour from an empty cup. In order to show up in the best possible way for your loved ones, your work, your clients or whoever else needs you, you've got to serve yourself first. Just as on a plane they instruct you to put on your own oxygen mask before you help others, the same idea can be applied here. Look after yourself first and you will be able to be the best mother/wife/friend/sister/co-worker/business owner/coach that you can be.

Taking inspired action is about making room not just for the things that bring you joy, but also the things that restore your energy and make you feel like the best version of you. These things have to become non-negotiable. I class my daily yoga practice as one of my daily business activities. It's as important as a client meeting or connecting with my team. Why? Because it helps me feel amazing and keeps me in the space of ease and flow, and it is from that place that I can manifest incredible wins. Whenever I've seen a dip in my income in my business, I can pretty much always connect it to a time when I'd neglected my own wellbeing and had reverted back to old patterns of behaviour by hustling too hard and not making myself a priority. Inspired action is about taking the steps towards your goals, whilst honouring your own desires, wants and needs.

"You don't need to see the whole staircase, just take the first step."~Martin Luther King

A question I do get asked a lot from people is "what if I don't know what action to take to get me closer to my desires? How can I take inspired action if I don't know what action to take? What if I don't know how to get to my destination?"

If you are faced with similar questions about your own path right now, I'd like to remind you that manifesting is a process of co-creation. It is a process where you and The Universe work in harmony together to create the life you want. While we need to take inspired action, we have to remember that there are an infinite number of ways for our desires to unfold. The "how" things will manifest is not entirely our concern. In the following chapter, we will discuss more about the importance of surrendering things to The Universe and allowing The Universe to work it's magic, but understand that how to get from where you are now to where you want to be isn't solely down to you. You don't have to have it all figured out right now, you simply need to do something, anything, that feels good, and that will inch you closer to the thing which you desire.

As Martin Luther King famously said, "You don't need to see the whole staircase, just take the first step." Once you start moving on your authentic path, having fun and doing the things that bring you joy, The Universe will step in to validate that path and will start sending you people, experiences and things that will nudge you towards the next action step to take. As you move forwards, the path will start to appear.

This is where it becomes incredibly important to pay attention to your own inner guidance system and the wisdom of The Universe when figuring out what you need to do next. So often, people will seek out advice from friends or family, or from experts to show them what to do and to tell them which action step to take next. Whilst I'm not denying that expert guidance can be incredibly powerful, it shouldn't mean that you cut yourself off from your own power in the process. When we hand over every decision in our life to others or when we constantly search for validation from others when it comes to making a choice on what we need to do next, we disempower ourselves and do not allow ourselves to hear what The Universe has to say.

Having someone to lead you in pursuit of your goals is great, but you need to remember that The Universe will send you signs along the way too and using your own intuition is a powerful way to tune in to those signs.

An example of this is within my own entrepreneurial journey. When I first started out as a coach, I had zero experience of running a business. I didn't fully understand how I was going to attract clients and make money. I couldn't see the whole staircase but I did take the first step and started to put a lot of energy into creating content, sharing posts on social media and making videos, knowing that this was something I really enjoyed doing.

I was longing to help and inspire others, and so that's what I started to show up and do. I was taking lots of inspired action, having huge amounts of fun within my business and focusing as much as possible on my core zone of genius. The parts of my business that I knew I just wouldn't enjoy figuring out, I decided to get some support with. I ended up signing up to a business program, and it was amazing to be led by someone who had already created the success I wanted to see.

For a while, I felt the benefits that the support of this program and the experts within it were having on my business. Then, a few weeks later, things began to shift. I started to feel a bit disconnected from my business and found myself lacking motivation. I couldn't figure out what it was until I realised that I'd stopped doing a lot of the things within my business I really loved.

For example, a part of the program had provided me with templates for creating copy, including pre-formatted social media posts and emails. Rather than writing my own content, something that was my core zone of genius and my way to take inspired action as a business owner, I started to integrate these templates into my business. These templates were meant to make my life easier, but instead, they were causing me to feel a lot of resistance within my business. I stopped showing up online as much as I was and didn't feel the same kind of desire to inspire others. I felt like my business had almost become a bit of a chore. I knew that the action I was taking had become far from inspired. I was so intent on following the guidance of the experts in the program, I totally shut myself off from my own magic and from the magic of The Universe. Once I re-connected to the things that brought me joy and got back into the flow of writing my own content, my business began to thrive.

Now again, I'm not saying that having expert support cannot be a huge benefit to you as you move towards your goals. Whether it's hiring a coach, a personal trainer, a business guru or anyone else, I'm hugely in support of having people in your life who can help you get to where you want to be faster. However, I don't believe we should put our whole lives into the hands of others and blindly be led. We often sell ourselves short by convincing ourselves we don't know the answers or what to do and sometimes, we need to trust ourselves a little bit more. A woman's intuition is a powerful thing. In fact, I believe it's our Super Power, yet so often we choose to ignore it.

We "Google" the answers, ask friends for advice or wait for someone else to tell us we are "good enough" to go for our dreams. But here's the thing: Inspired Action doesn't come from someone else telling us what to do. Inspired Action is when we give ourselves permission to do the things that make our heart sing, trusting that when we are having fun, things are always unfolding in our favour.

We all know at least one thing, even if it feels tiny, that we could be doing right now that will edge us closer to our dreams. If you have a desire to start a business but have no clue what business to start, Inspired Action could be spending an hour researching other women in business and reading stories from other inspiring entrepreneurs to see how they got started. If you want to manifest your soulmate, what fun things could you do that could open you up to meeting new people? Inspired Action in this scenario may be booking in for a class you've always wanted to take or going to grab a coffee at the new coffee place you had your eye on.

When you start taking even the tiniest of steps in the right direction, steps that feel good to you, you will find that the next logical step will start to appear. The Universe will start to send people, experiences and things into your life to guide you and support you in having your desires. You take one step, and The Universe takes the next. Your intuition knows what you need to do first, so start listening to it!

Use the exercise below, and I challenge you to not come up with at least one inspired action step that you could take right now that will help you to move closer to your desires.

Inspired Action Exercise

Think about one desire you have right now. Choose a desire you've been thinking about for a while and write it down. Now, I invite you to think about how many times have you convinced yourself you don't know how to get to that desire? How many times have you assumed you'd need someone else to show you the way? How many times have you felt you don't have the solution to achieving this desire?

Now, I would like you to think about that desire and write down one thing you can do right now that will move you closer towards that goal and is something that you enjoy doing? Listen to your heart here.

Don't get too caught up in your head or worry about whether what you write down is wrong or right.

Simply write down any answers that pops up that brings you joy.

Take a few minutes to brainstorm on this and I challenge you to not come up with at least one thing that you could do over the next week.

Surrender

Surrender to what is. Let go of what was. Have faith in what will be. ~ Sonia Ricotti

So far on this path to true Self Love and manifesting the life of our wildest dreams, we have covered the importance of:

- Getting clarity on your desires and letting The Universe know what it is you want.
- Identifying what beliefs are keeping us stuck.
- Doing the work to transform negative beliefs and create a new set of beliefs that match the reality that you want to create.
- Releasing negative energy and raising your vibration so that you become a vibrational match to your desires.
- Taking Inspired Action towards the life you want.

So what is next?

This is where we step into possibly the hardest part of the process. This is where we hand things over to The Universe and surrender ourselves completely. This is where we let go. In theory, this should be the easiest thing to do as it requires nothing on our part. We don't need to do more, we just need to allow The Universe to work it's magic. The reality however, is that it's letting go that many struggle with the most.

This is hands down the hardest part of the process for me because I'm a self-proclaimed control freak. I like to be in the driving seat and call the shots. I like to keep an eye on what is happening. In fact, it took me ages to make my first hire in my business and even when I did, I found myself micromanaging. I couldn't just let things be and what this really boiled down to was that I didn't have enough trust and faith that things would work without my input.

The same was true when it came to co-creating with The Universe. I fully believed (and of course still do believe) in the powers of The Universe, but a part of me wanted to keep tabs on what The Universe was up to. I felt like I had to be constantly involved in the process, so I'd keep checking in to see when the money would appear or when the clients would come, and when I still didn't see evidence, I became impatient. *"Hello! Universe? I've asked for some clients. Where are they?"*

Of course, what I didn't realise was this impatience was actually pushing my desires further away. When we become impatient, this is typically when we start to push for things, or will for things to happen. This is where we start to force things. This is where we start to hustle and start acting from a place of desperation. This kind of action then pushes us further out of alignment with our goals. Think about things you've tried to force in your life, a relationship, for example. Does it make you feel good? Rarely.

At the time of writing this paragraph, I am just sixteen weeks post my emergency C-section. A few days ago, I decided I was ready to get back onto the yoga mat and into my regular yoga practice. Once back on my mat, it didn't take me long to realise that I was not moving in the same way I used to, nor did I have the same kind of flexibility. Wanting to yoga how I used to yoga, I overdid it on one of the poses, a pose which required a level of hamstring stretch that I no longer seemed to possess. Rather than knowing my limits and being gentle with myself, I tried to yank my leg back even further into the pose, forcing my leg to go as far as it could. At this point, an awful pain shot up my leg. It felt like I'd torn the whole muscle in half. I ended up not being able to go to another session for a whole week.

Forcing things rarely feels good and more often than not, it pushes us further away from our desired outcome. I went to start back at yoga to help my body heal and to re-energise myself, but by forcing things, I ended up wounding it and feeling exhausted.

This is what happens when we don't surrender to the process and let go. I should have surrendered into the pose, recognised my limits and then let go. I tried to push myself rather than allow things to happen. I tried to force myself to do more, to be more and ultimately, this didn't lead anywhere. When we refuse to surrender and let go, we stop The Universe from working its magic.

I've witnessed the most amazing experiences in the moments when I've fully surrendered to the process. One particular example of this was a trip I took to Greece. Normally, when going on holidays in the past, I would meticulously plan everything, wanting to make the most of every second of the day. I'd plan where we'd visit, where we'd eat, what activities we'd do. Nothing was left to guess work. Then the holiday would come and it almost felt like it wasn't a holiday at all. It was a process of getting things done, ticking things off a list. I would struggle to relax and just enjoy the ride and my time off.

Then, on this particular trip to Greece, I decided I would surrender to the experience, go with the flow and let The Universe guide me. Very little plans were made. There was space for being spontaneous. There was space for things to just unfold. I remember one day, we stumbled across the most amazing little beach bar, hidden away off the beaten path.

While we were there, I got chatting with a woman, and it turned out that she worked within the coaching industry too. We ended up spending the afternoon sipping on cocktails together talking about all things Law of Attraction, mindset, crystals, basically all of my favourite things to talk about! She also told me about an amazing retreat that she had recently been on, which sounded just like something I'd been searching for. The trip turned out to be one of the best trips I've ever had. Amazing places, experiences and people showed up in my life sent by The Universe because I'd allowed The Universe to support me and guide me. I'd allowed The Universe to work its magic too.

Here's the thing: Manifesting is a process of CO-CREATION. There are countless ways to reach your desires but to get there, you've got to let go of the idea that getting to where you want to go has to look a certain way. When you try and control every tiny detail and take over the how and the when your desires will manifest, you deny The Universe its chance to play its role and work its magic.

Self Love is about allowing yourself to let go and be supported. When you LET GO, you create space for The Universe to step in and assist you by sending you people, experiences, opportunities and things that will help you in living your highest version of life. So give The Universe a little bit of slack, loosen those reins and allow yourself to be guided.

You cannot struggle to what you want. It has to be easy ~ Abraham Hicks

What is beautiful about surrendering is that when you let go, you allow things to be easy. Think about where in your life are you trying to force things. Is it helping? Has it allowed you to reach your goals? Or has it made the whole process feel like an uphill struggle? We make life far more difficult than what it needs to be when we assume that we are the only one responsible for getting to our goals.

Surrendering is about being patient with where you're at right now, trusting that you are being supported in your path. When we assume the entire responsibility for our goals, it's easy to then place the entire blame on ourselves if things don't work out. For me, being kind and gentle with myself as I am in the process of manifesting my desires has become a huge part of practicing true Self Love. When I get impatient, I'm rarely kind to myself. I can hear myself saying things such as: "You should have succeeded by now" "Maybe it's not going to happen for you." "You just need to work harder" My response is then to push myself even further. I kill any joy from the process because it becomes more about getting to the goal than it is about enjoying the journey.

In contrast, when I fully surrender to The Universe, there is no blame mentality. I don't beat myself when things don't work out or move slower than expected because I know, I've already done my bit. I know that I'm not the only one responsible for my desires. I put my trust in the hands of The Universe and know that my role is to continue to love where I'm at now, love myself and the woman I'm becoming and have faith that everything I desire is already on it's way.

It's not something we often associate with Self Love, but having patience with the process is a hugely powerful way to practice it. Not only does impatience encourage us to revert back to the negative self-talk and a lack of Self Love, but impatience also demonstrates a loss of faith. When you are impatient to receive your desires, you are acting from a place of fear over love and in doing so, you put yourself out of alignment. The message you are sending out is "I need physical proof that my desires exist and I'll only relax and be happy when I have what I physically want in my hands"

But here's the thing: You have to be showing up as if the physical manifestation of what you want is already with you. You have to be as happy now as you would be when your desires manifest. So let's say for example you order something online, and it gets delivered the next day. Would you continue to sit by the door and wait impatiently for the parcel? No, because you know it's already been delivered. You'd be out there living your life. The same is true for your desires. You need to act as if they've already arrived, because in some ways, they already have. Maybe they've not physically manifested yet, but your desires are out there. The only thing that is stopping them from physically appearing is because you are being impatient and holding them apart from you. Patience is the key to getting what you want, and you will need it because of what I refer to as the "manifestation gap".

The manifestation gap is the period of time between asking for what you want, doing the inner work, taking inspired action and then the receiving of your desires. Sometimes, things will feel like they manifest instantaneously. Most of the time, however, there will be a gap.

So why does this gap exist and what purpose does it serve? Well firstly, this gap exists because you've already set into motion prior manifestations that have to play out first. So if you've been thinking negatively your whole life, there may be some unwanted things that you may experience before the wanted manifestations begin to appear. In fact, a lot of my clients report that things get worse before they get better and that's ok! Typically, it means you're on the right path and that you're in the receptive mode. When you start doing this work, you start to dig up a lot of junk (old beliefs, negative energy, unwanted emotions). As you dig these up, you may experience a few unwanted physical manifestations in the process. You've got to ride that wave out.

Also, remember that it's not always in our best interests for things to manifest instantaneously. Imagine if every time you thought a negative thought it physically manifested before your eyes? So let's say that for a split second, you thought "my house is going to burn down" and then it did. The gap here is beneficial because it allows you to recognise negative thought patterns and change them before they snowball out of control and start to lead to unwanted things or events.

The manifestation gap is also there to serve you on a personal level in that the waiting game can actually ignite some positive changes in who you are. Sometimes we need to become the woman we need to be to get us to where we want to go, and it's in the waiting that our biggest breakthroughs occur. I know one thousand per cent that I would not be the person I am today if everything I wanted had just dropped into my lap and had come easily and instantly.

Often, my biggest wins have come off the back of times when I've felt like I'd been waiting forever for things to change. It's in the waiting that we learn new truths about ourselves, test our faith, get out of our comfort zones, deepen our spiritual practice and strengthen our tenacity.

Take for instance, one of my business goals of hitting six figures in one month. It had been something I'd asked The Universe for and had done my part in the process in that I had worked on my beliefs and energy and was taking lots of inspired action. The only thing left for me to do was to wait. Achieving my goal certainly didn't happen overnight. In fact, it took much longer for me to hit that goal than I would have liked.

During the wait, however, I never once questioned that the Universe would show up and support me. I knew if I could maintain this faith, everything would work out how I wanted it to. Interestingly, it was during that waiting game that I had some of my biggest shifts both on a spiritual and personal level and on a business level.

The waiting game made me reconsider some of the ways I was running my business, and it was during this time I launched a new program that has gone on to become our most successful program to date. During the waiting game, I also doubled down on my own mindset work and in doing so, further strengthened my self worth and discovered some new spiritual rituals that have now become a huge part of my daily practice. During the waiting game, I also forced myself to get out of my comfort zone by hiring more team members who have now become an integral part of our growth.

I don't look back and think "it was so annoying that I had to wait for so long for my goal to manifest." I don't look at the waiting game as time wasted. I look at it, and I see it as a time where I learned incredible amounts about myself, my business, who I wanted to be and the empire I wanted to create.

The manifestation gap can be a magical thing if you allow it, but this is only possible when you are firm in your belief that things are always working out for you. I'm a huge believer in divine timing. We have to surrender to the "when" our desires are to manifest and trust that they will appear when it is in our best interests, and at the exact moment we are meant to receive them.

Our role is to get clear on what we want, do the inner work to change our beliefs and raise our energy and then take lots of inspired action but once we've done that, it's then time for The Universe to play its part. This is, after all, a process of co-creating. The Universe's role in the process is to deliver your desires when you are meant to receive them and to provide you with the people, circumstances and resources that you need for your desires to come to life.

When you will receive your desires is up to The Universe and while you can give The Universe some indication about timing, you have to fully trust that what you want is coming and expect it to land into your life at any given moment. This requires three things. One, faith and two patience, and three, the ability to detach from the outcome.

Let's start with patience as it's something we've already touched upon and I know that patience isn't always easy. We live in a fast-paced world where we can get everything we want with the click of a button and it will be delivered to us the next day, sometimes within a few hours. Or think about when a new show comes out on Netflix.

We don't have to wait weekly for each episode. We can binge watch it all in one go. Nowadays, we don't have to wait for anything and because of this, waiting for our desires to appear can be difficult. We aren't used to practising patience.

Patience, however, is like a muscle. The more we use it, the stronger it becomes, and patience is something we need by the bucketload to keep ourselves in alignment. When we become impatient, we show that our faith is wavering, that we are starting to doubt. These doubts create uncertainty, and this uncertainty makes us feel uncomfortable and uncomfortable is not a high vibe place to be. We don't attract what we "hope" will manifest. We attract what we "know" will manifest. As soon as you cast doubt on your desires, you hold them further away from you.

One thing I like to tell my clients to help them be patient is this: What if the wait exists because The Universe is preparing to deliver to you something far greater than you ever imagined? If you know what incredible things are in store for you, you wouldn't mind the wait. Often, the best things are those things we've had to wait for and often, the things we receive are all the more joyful because we've had to wait for them.

At the time of writing, I've yet to manifest my dream house. This is by far my "biggest" desire and the one that excites me the most. Whilst it would be wonderful for this house to be in my possession right now, I fully trust one day it will be, and I don't mind waiting as once I get it, it will be so incredible that any waiting would pale in comparison.

Another question I like to ask my clients is: Would you rather receive £1000 tomorrow? Or one million in three years? Ninety per cent of my clients tell me they'd rather wait for the one million. You see, if we dig deeper, we realise that waiting is rarely the issue. We can be patient with things we are certain about. The issue is the wavering of faith while we wait. We can be patient with the things we know are certain to arrive, and we wait for them with excitement. Take, for example, booking a holiday. We eagerly and excitedly wait for the holiday to arrive. The waiting game feels fun when we have no doubts about getting to our desired destination. Impatience and frustration appear when we start to doubt whether our desires will arrive at all.

This is where faith comes in. Faith is about knowing with every inch of your being that The Universe is conspiring to give you all that you've asked for and is in the process of delivering it to you. Imagine you've received a check from a friend that you've cashed in at the bank. The money doesn't appear in your account straight away but you know it's coming. You aren't ringing the bank up every five minutes asking when the money will appear. You trust it will come.

The same is true for your desires. You have to expect them to arrive to the point you'd be surprised if they don't because your faith that The Universe is going to deliver is that strong. When your faith is unshakeable, you are not spending your time worrying about whether or not things will work out for you. Instead, you let go and enjoy the ride. This leads me to detaching from the outcome.

In my life, nothing goes wrong. When things seem to not meet my expectations, I let go of how I think things should be. It's a matter of not having any attachment to any fixed outcome. ~ Deepak Chopra.

Letting go means detaching completely from the outcome, which feels a bit confusing given that we are also supposed to focus on our desires and our goals and get specific about what we want.

How do we both think about what we want yet simultaneously detach from the outcome? How are we supposed to get excited about our goals as if they are already present, yet at the same time, forget about them completely? I believe the key here (and what has worked for myself and many of my clients since) is the art of mindfulness and being in the present.

Presence is when you're no longer waiting for the next moment, believing that the next moment will be more fulfilling than this one. ~ Eckhart Tolle.

One of the books I read when I was in my rock bottom was *"The Power of Now"* by Eckharte Tolle. At the time I thought mindfulness was a useful tool for helping me to feel better. I could let go of the pain of what was going on in my life and focus on the now and on the current moment. As I did this, I felt peace. I felt a calmness I'd not felt in a while. What I didn't appreciate at this point was the role mindfulness could play in helping me manifest anything I wanted.

Mindfulness is about living in the present. It's about detaching from the past and the future knowing that the only moment that really matters is the one we are in right now and this is so important. You see, in between where you are now and where you want to get to is a thing called "life" that is meant to be lived and enjoyed to the fullest and that life is happening right now.

People say "I'll be happy when" but how about trying "I'll be happy now" and enjoy this very moment for what it is? Mindfulness for me is about finding as much joy as you can in the now, without overthinking what has been or what is yet to come. When you are so occupied with living your best life right here right now, you have little time to think about what you don't yet have. You become detached from the outcome because you're not thinking about what is coming in the future, but focusing on the joy of the now.

But what if you feel like there is little to be joyful about in your physical world? My solution here is to create it in your mind. Our minds are more powerful than we realise and sometimes, it can feel just as magical to think about our desires as it is to physically experience them. Just close your eyes for a few minutes. Where in the world would you love to be right now and who with? What are you doing? Create an image so vivid that it feels real. Go to that place for a few minutes and while you are there, savour it as if it's your current reality. How do you feel?

Know that this feeling is available to you at any given moment. You can choose how to feel in the now and when you choose joy, you no longer fixate on what you don't yet have. You surrender to what is and let go of what is to come and it's from this space that you open yourself up to receiving the gifts from The Universe.

So patience, faith and detaching from the outcome are all necessary parts of creating our dream life, but practising these things isn't always easy, and often, it feels like we're being tested. When things don't show up when we ask for them or unwanted manifestations come our way, it can sometimes feel like we've done something wrong or that The Universe doesn't yet see us worthy of what we are asking for. This is not the case. There is nothing we need to prove about ourselves in order to receive our desires. We are worthy just as we are and it is our birthright to live our fullest life possible. The only thing we need to demonstrate is our faith.

One game I like to play to help me strengthen my faith that The Universe is going to deliver is to pay attention to all of life's little synchronicities. The Universe is constantly providing us with little nudges to remind us that what we want is on its way. We just need to make sure we are paying attention.

Take, for instance, a client of mine who wanted to manifest her dream car, a white Mercedes convertible. She let The Universe know what she wanted, she pinned it to her vision board, she spoke affirmations about it already being in her possession, she created the feelings as if she already had it by going out to test drive it. She started researching local dealerships to find out what cars were available. Within a week of doing this, she began to see her dream car everywhere. She saw one drive past her as she came out of her house one morning. She found one parked beside her as she came out of the shops.

Every time she saw one of these cars, she took it as a sign from The Universe that hers was on the way. With each sighting, her faith strengthened. Then, one day, she was looking out of her office window at the carpark that it faced onto and sure enough, there in the carpark was the dream car, only it had on the window a sign which she could read clearly. It said "For Sale".

Nipping out to take a closer look, she decided to give the number on the sign a call to enquire about the car. She waited as the phone rang, knowing with every inch of her being that the car was already hers until eventually, someone picked up. "Oh I'm so sorry," the person told her. "The car was sold this morning. Someone rang me up today and said they want to buy it for their wife. I've just not had a chance to take the sign down."

Now rather than become disappointed, impatient or frustrated like many of us would, my client chose to respond with faith and see this as another message from The Universe that her car was so close she could almost smell the fresh leather. Rather than getting angry, she thanked The Universe for giving her such a huge sign that what she wants is coming and felt excitement surge through her. She reconnected with her feeling of that car already being in her possession and knew it very soon would be. Getting home from work that night, what did she see sitting in her driveway? Yep, that's right. Her white Mercedes convertible dream car. It had been her husband that had made the call that morning. He was the secret buyer.

When she told me this story, it gave me goosebumps. There is nothing more exhilarating than hearing people recall their experiences of The Law of Attraction working in their favour. Pay attention to the signs from The Universe that what you want is on its way. Keep an eye open for subtle hints connected to your desires and when you recognise these messages, give thanks to The Universe as if your desire is already yours. The secret to having it all, is having 100% faith that you already do.

Exercise - The 24 hour Surrender Game

I like to think of this exercise as a game as I think when it comes to detaching, things should be playful. Play helps keep us in the energy of detachment. Play keeps things light and easy. Play around with this exercise for the next 24 hours and see where it takes you.

Don't get too fixated on any specific outcome but revel in the uncertainty of what The Universe will deliver. To play this game, commit to one twenty four hour period where you will completely hand things over to The Universe.

Go about your day making as few plans as possible and just be guided by what you feel called to do. If something doesn't go to plan, rather than getting frustrated, remind yourself that The Universe is unfolding things in your favour and trust that things are happening for a reason.

During this 24 hour period, there is no end goal to get to, or rather there is, but that is for The Universe to know and for you to find out.

Allow The Universe to take the wheel as you become the passenger and see what magic appears for you. Keep a journal to help you document all of the tiny little miracles that show up for you over the course of your day.

Embracing Your Feminine Energy

The union of feminine and masculine energies within the individual is the basis for all creation ~ Shakti Gawain

The final part of the process to cultivate Self Love and step into the woman we are meant to be so that we can manifest anything we desire is all to do with our Feminine Energy. In order to rise up at the goddesses that we truly are, we must honour our feminine energy and allow it the space it needs to breathe life into us and allow us to shine in the brightest possible way.

This feminine energy is a powerful force, and when we embrace it, we can harness this energy to carry us closer to our desires. But what exactly is feminine energy? You may be assuming that feminine energy has something to do with being a woman, however, this is not quite true. Both feminine and masculine energies are present both in men and in women and to live in the most harmonious and joyful way possible, it requires that there is the right balance of both of these forces. Just like yin and yang, you need both energies: they complement each other.

Feminine Energy is all about Self Love, being guided by your intuition, being in the flow, compassion, collaboration and simply just being, rather than doing. It's also about allowing yourself to be vulnerable, a topic I'm hugely passionate about. In contrast, Masculine Energy is much more action orientated. It's about getting things done, it's about producing, it's about pushing for things, it's about competing.

The thing is, much of modern society is led by this Masculine Energy. Think about how most major corporations and governments run. Employees are encouraged to work hard to climb their career ladder. Politicians push and compete for power. As a society, we are goal and action-focused, always striving to progress and to innovate rather than to simply be here in the now and allow nature to take its course. Our to-do lists often come before our own self care. We rarely allow ourselves time to create and play for the pure reason that it brings us joy. A lot of what we do is attached to some sort of end goal.

While many of the traits of Masculine Energy can serve us and in fact, some of the amazing things we enjoy as a society may have not been created without the masculine energy, it's important to not get so caught up in the masculine that we forget to nurture our feminine sides. When we activate our Feminine Energy, we give ourselves permission to bloom in our most authentic way and a way that keeps us in alignment with our true selves.

For many women, residing too much in their Masculine Energy doesn't feel good. When we push or force for things, try to compete with others, don't allow time for self-care, ignore our desire to create or disconnect from others, we detach ourselves from the feminine and put ourselves out of alignment. Then, when we are out of alignment, it becomes very difficult to become the women we are meant to be or manifest the things we want to manifest. Activating our feminine energy then is crucial if we want to fully step into our power and create the life of our wildest dreams.

One of the first proper jobs I had upon graduating Law School was working in the legal department of one of the world's largest Stockbrokers. To begin with, working in this incredible skyscraper within such a fast paced, buzzy industry felt exciting. After a while, however, something didn't feel quite right and I began to get increasingly unhappy in my work environment.

I couldn't put my finger on it at the time, but now I realise it was because this kind of environment was nudging me out of my feminine energy and too much into the masculine. Within the company, Masculine Energy was the dominant force. This was not only evidenced by the fact that the majority of the company's employees were male, but also in that the work culture was very much a masculine vibe.

Everyone saw working hard as this thing to be proud of and wore their ability to hustle late into the evening as a badge of honor. There was very much a "go big or go home" kind of mentality. As it happens, I decided to "go home" and never return. I remember when I quit this job, I felt angry with myself for not being able to hack it but deep down, I knew that it was the right decision. I felt that being in this role was turning me into someone I wasn't and I knew that if I stayed long enough, it would suck me in, and I may never have escaped.

This isn't to say that every corporate company has the same level of masculinity within their company culture and I do think that things are beginning to shift. However, from what I hear from friends who are still in the corporate world, masculine energy still is the dominating force, as is the case for much of our society. Because of this, it's important that we nurture our Feminine Energy as often as we can and allow ourselves time and space for our goddess energy to come to life.

The work I personally needed to do on myself in order to balance my own energies became evident when I first started my business. It had become very apparent that the masculine energy of the corporate world was something I was struggling to let go of. I had started my business in the hope I could live a different pace of life. I wanted more freedom, more time for myself and self-care. I wanted to work in a more relaxed way.

Coming into my business, I found myself quickly slipping into my Masculine Energy, buying into the hustle, working incredibly long hours and being so fixated on my goals for my business that it got to a point where everything felt forced and an uphill struggle. I was still clinging onto an identity of what I thought success should look like, this identity being a product of the masculine corporate society in which I'd previously worked in. For a while, I held onto a belief that the only way for my business to grow and for me to lead, was through adopting this very masculine way of being. I soon realised, however, that this energy was actually holding me back from really thriving as a business owner and coach. It wasn't until I started to honour and activate my Feminine Energy that things really began to shift for me in a powerful way.

The shift was not just in how I felt, but also in what I received. Once I allowed space for my Feminine Energy, I witnessed success and money began to pour into my business with ease. Ironically, I had assumed that doing more would get me to where I wanted to go but incidentally, what I needed to do was less. Rather than push for more, I needed to allow for more to flow into my life.

Our Feminine Energy should not be mistaken as weak. Do not assume that connecting with the feminine means we have to give up on our goals, but rather, we approach these goals from a different perspective. Rather than forcing things to happen, we allow things to come to us. This ties in with what we discussed during the previous chapter on the importance of surrender, which is one way in which we can honour the feminine.

Surrendering means letting go of forcing things or trying to push for things, and as we do so, we ignite the feminine within us. But how else can we nurture our feminine energy? To be honest, to go into an in depth discussion of the Feminine Energy is probably the topic for another book, but let me share with you some of the ways I've helped myself, and subsequently my clients embrace their feminine energy, so that they can unleash their inner goddess and rise up as the empowered, successful and abundant women they are today.

Movement

Dance like no one is watching ~ Mark Twain

Let's start with going back to the morning ritual I discussed at the beginning of this book and think about movement. One thing that I urge you all to do each morning as part of your daily ritual is to move. It doesn't need to be a full workout. You could start with a few yoga sun salutations or simply just dance around your room to your favourite music. Whatever works for you. Feminine Energy is a moving energy. Things in nature that are in constant motion such as the ocean, hurricanes, and weather patterns are all perfect examples of the Feminine Energy at work. While there are no doubt countless health benefits of exercise, movement is also a powerful way to ignite the feminine within you and as you do, you will feel yourself shift into your power.

Moving feels good, especially if you work in a role where you are stuck at a desk. This type of movement I'm talking about, however, isn't a goal-orientated movement. This isn't about improving at something or trying to impress someone. This is moving for the pure fact that it brings you joy. Remember that to be driven by goals and to push for a certain outcome is very much a masculine trait. This isn't about trying to lose weight or trying to run a certain distance or to achieve some sort of fitness goal.

This type of movement is purely about allowing your feminine energy to be awakened. It's about feeling and being right here right now without worrying about where the movement will lead. It's about fully embracing who you are in the present, rather than being driven by some ulterior motive.

A great type of movement for this is Dance. Dancing and moving without thinking, following the impulses of the body, allows the flowing nature of the wild feminine to pulse through you. There is no purpose behind the movement other than for you to feel joy, to feel alive. Dance like no one's watching for a few minutes each morning and see how you feel.

Create

While the Masculine Energy is destructive, the feminine is creative. As children, we spend so much time creating for the pure joy of creating yet as adults, many of us don't make enough space for this. When we suppress our creative desires, we deny the Feminine Energy within us.

There are countless ways in which we can express our creativity. As part of becoming a coach, much of my work now involves creating content, and one of my biggest passions is writing. Whether this is writing content for my audience, my clients or even this book, writing is something that brings me huge amounts of joy.

It is, however, important that you find ways to create that aren't attached to some sort of end goal. Remember that the feminine is about being rather than doing. You need to find ways to create which are not intended to get you to some sort of outcome such as a business goal.

How you unleash your creativity is up to you. Play around with different things until you find your sweet spot. It could be painting or drawing, writing poetry, learning an instrument or even playing with childhood games such as lego. One thing I love to guide my clients to help them activate their feminine power is Creative Journaling. See below for some Creative Journaling prompts.

Exercise - Creative Journaling

Take your journal and go to your sacred space where you won't be disturbed.

It is essential that your journal be kept confidential so that you are not worrying about the judgment or criticism of others. The process is intended to ignite your creativity rather than stifle it. Find a safe place to keep your journal.

If others can read or see your journal, then you will find yourself filtering your thoughts rather than allowing them to just flow.

Use the following journal prompts to guide you through the Creative Journaling Process.

Journal prompt one

Draw how you feel right now. After the drawing is completed, write about what is in the picture.

Journal prompt two

Create a drawing about what kind of day you are having, and why? After the drawing is completed, write about what is in the picture.

Journal prompt three

Create a drawing of your favourite colour, place, food, book, song, or movie. After the drawing is completed, write about what is in the picture.

Journal prompt four

Create a drawing about what you like to do? How does it make you feel? After the drawing is completed, write about what is in the picture. Journal prompt five Create a drawing about where you are happiest? After the drawing is completed, write about what is in the picture.

Embracing Vulnerability

Allowing ourselves to be vulnerable is not easy. It is, however, essential if we are to fully step into our feminine power. Through the lens of a society driven by masculine forces, vulnerability can be viewed as a weakness when in fact, embracing vulnerability and therefore our Feminine Energy is strength. Let's take a look though at what being vulnerable really means.

There is a crack, a crack in everything. That's how the light gets in.~ Leonard Cohen

Allowing yourself to be vulnerable means letting go of perfectionism and the pressure we put on ourselves to be the best we can be and do the best we can do. Now I know this book is all about improving your life and becoming the best version of you, but I don't want you to mistake this with perfectionism. I'm not here to help you try and create the perfect life or become a perfect person because I don't believe perfect exists and even if it did, I don't believe it would serve us.

We need the road bumps just as much as we need the wins, for it is in the moments of failure or hardship that we learn some of the biggest lessons about ourselves. Don't be fooled into thinking that perfectionism creates a perfect life. It doesn't. It creates stress. It causes you to compete and compare. It puts unnecessary pressure on you. It stifles your Feminine Energy rather than igniting it.

Perfectionism is largely about trying to earn the approval of others. Maybe you consider yourself as a perfectionist and if so, think about how you have grown up. Did you find yourself being praised for achievements and how well you performed? Maybe this was in school, in sports or maybe even in your appearance? When there is constant praise for a specific area of your life, you develop a belief that your worth is attached to what you achieve.

You believe that you have to perform to be accepted. You come to believe that what you do and how perfectly you do it will determine the approval you receive from loved ones or society.

This is different from self-improvement. Self-improvement is about wanting to do you for you, rather trying to please other people. Self-improvement isn't attached to external validation. Perfectionism, on the other hand, is all about what 'they' think and when we are led too much by what others think of us, we find ourselves pushing for certain things, over striving, working too hard, doing too much, all in the quest of being "perfect".

When we deny our emotion, it owns us.~ Brene Brown

Vulnerability is also about owning our emotions, something I've admittedly struggled with in the past. Remember my wild and crazy days of shopping like a mad woman that I told you about earlier in this book? I initially thought that the reason for my addiction to shopping was simply because I loved clothes (and shoes, and bags...) Since I've done a lot of work on myself, however, I've actually realised I don't really love shopping as much as I thought I did. While I do like to give attention to what I wear and love to wear things that make me feel good, there is now a very long list of things I'd prefer to do over storm up and down Oxford Circus, credit card at the ready.

The truth is, my love of shopping wasn't the issue. The issue was that I was using shopping to avoid having to deal with my emotions. At the time, I was caught up in sadness, anger, jealousy and low confidence and rather than tackle these feelings head-on, I numbed them out through shopping. I was numbing the pain of feeling "not enough" in my career and in my relationship. I didn't want to confront these negative emotions because I thought to do so would be too painful and difficult, so instead, I chose to ignore them entirely and numb them out through my shopping addiction.

Do you resonate with this at all? How are you choosing to numb yourself whether it through shopping, drinking, binge-watching Netflix or some other "addiction"? Now you may be thinking "but if what I focus on expands and I'm to keep my vibe high to manifest positive things into my life, shouldn't I numb myself to these negative emotions?"

Here's the thing: You can't be selective over which emotions you choose to allow and when you numb out negative emotions, you also numb yourself to the good ones too. This emotional indifference was something I myself experienced. While I was shopping like a maniac and numbing out my own feelings of inadequacy, I was also dulling any feelings of excitement or joy. Nothing seemed to excite me anymore, and I became half-hearted about the stuff that once lit me up.

Remember that feeling good and experiencing joy is so important for manifesting our desires, but we can only fully experience the good when we allow ourselves to feel the bad. There needs to be cracks for the light to come in.

It's therefore essential for us to be able to acknowledge the negative but then subsequently release those emotions and not dwell on them. When you dwell on the negative, you experience more negative. But when you brush the negative emotions under the carpet, they linger and stagnate and end up doing more harm than good. What's more, is that this avoidance of emotions actually shifts us out of our Feminine Energy and therefore our power. What we need to do then, is embrace our emotions, the good, the bad and the ugly, honour them and then let them go.

A good place to start is by looking at certain patterns of behaviour you find yourself falling into and ask yourself WHY you are doing that thing. So let's say for example, drinking wine in the evening when you get home from work is your fix. Be honest with yourself about why you're doing it. Do you have one glass and savour the taste and it leaves you feeling great? Or do you find yourself polishing off a bottle without even really realising it and it leaves you feeling empty and numb? Are you doing it as a way to tune in with what you love, or to zone out?

Being overly emotional is something that our masculine society very much discourages. If we get angry, we get called crazy. If we cry, we are viewed as weak. We translate emotional as being dramatic or temperamental and as such, we are often so quick to run away from negative feelings rather than being present with them. Acknowledging our emotions, however, and embracing your feelings rather than denying them, is one of the most powerful practices you can learn if you want your feminine energy to be ignited.

Below is an exercise to help you identify and deal with emotions in a way that leaves you feeling empowered.

Step One: Identify the Emotion

The first step is to identify the emotion you are experiencing. If you struggle with this, pay attention to what the physical body is telling you as the body often leaves clues. What kind of physical sensations are you feeling and what thoughts are you having?

Try and then give a name to those sensations. If there are a few emotions, start by selecting the emotion you are feeling the most right now.

Once you have a name for the emotion, write it down on a slip of paper.

Step Two: Create Space

Once you have identified and named the emotion, close your eyes and imagine putting that emotion a few metres in front of you. For just a few minutes, imagine that you are going to place the emotion outside of your physical body so that you can look at it.

Step Three: Give the Emotion a Physical Form

Once the emotion is out of your body and in front of you, close your eyes and answer the following questions: If your emotion had a size, what size would it be? If your emotion had a shape, what shape would it be? If your emotion had a colour, what colour would it be?

Once you've answered these questions, imagine the emotion out in front of you with the size, shape, and colour you gave it. Just watch it for a few moments and recognise it for what it is. When you are ready, you can let the emotion return to its original place inside you.

Step Four: Reflect

Once you've finished steps one to three, reflect on what you noticed about your experience. Was there a change in the emotion when you created some distance from it? What about changes in your reactions to the emotion? What size, shape, and colour did you give the emotion? Did the emotion feel different in some way once the exercise was finished?

Practice this exercise daily for the next week and see if you notice any changes in how you relate to your emotions. Many of my clients have reported that this exercise helps them to become much more accepting of their emotions.

Tuning in with your natural rhythms

Nothing in nature blooms all year so don't expect yourself to either.

Do you sometimes ever feel like you have infinite amounts of energy, motivation and enthusiasm, yet at other times you can feel totally "meh"? Have you ever found yourself waking up feeling like you can take on the world, but other days feel like pulling the duvet over your head and calling it a "sick day"? In those times when you'd rather retreat, do nothing and nap, how often have you beaten yourself up for feeling this way?

How many times have you "got on with it" despite not feeling in the mood? Our energy, our motivation, our confidence levels, our productivity, these all ebb and flow, yet often we try to act as if they are constant, working in a way that ignores our own natural rhythms.

While Masculine Energy is very much a linear approach, about getting from A to B and getting it done, embracing your feminine energy means to go with the flow. This is something we discussed earlier in the chapter on surrender, but I want to now take this a little further and share with you how you can tune into and go with the flow of your natural cycles to ignite your feminine essence and ultimately, use this feminine power to manifest your desires.

Whilst your monthly visit from Aunt Flo (a.k.a your monthly period) may not have been something you'd have expected to read about in a book about Self Love and The Law of Attraction we are going there because let me tell you something; Since I started paying attention to my monthly cycle, I have found a new way of living and working that makes me feel amazing, expansive and has helped me become a magnet for some pretty incredible manifestations.

In Ancient Times, when a woman experienced her monthly period, it was believed that this was her wisdom was at its strongest and she possessed powers of creation and spiritual guidance. It was during the time of her month that other members of her community would look to her for guidance. Society then saw a shift into patriarchal views, and when a woman was bleeding, she was seen as impure and restricted from certain activities including attending church. While in modern society, many women still experience deep spiritual connections during their time of the month, it's not really a time that women celebrate.

So far we've focused on manifestation as a mind led concept. You think, and then you create, however, the mind and body are intrinsically linked, and manifestation is very much both a mind and body concept. Honouring the cycle of your physical body can actually have a huge positive knock-on effect on what you can manifest.

In fact, the first month I started paying attention to this work and allowed myself to be guided by my own natural rhythms, I witnessed a whole host of incredible things flow into my life. Stumbling into this work actually happened by accident while I was trying to find a book on tracking your cycle because my partner and I had decided we wanted to try for a baby. I'd previously never really paid attention to my period other than that I knew to stock up on chocolate for the time when my Aunt Flo came to visit. I knew that understanding my cycle and ovulation dates was important if I wanted to maximise my chances of conceiving.

What I soon discovered, however, was that tracking your cycle is not just useful for the art of baby-making, but also can be a powerful manifestation tool. While paying more attention to what phase of my monthly cycle I was in and how far I was until my next ovulation date, I also started to honour the different phases of my cycle. I allowed myself to be guided by these phases, rather than resisting them.

So for example, during menstruation, I'd spend more time retreating within my sacred space. I allowed for more time to meditate and just "be". I'd keep to environments that were soft, quiet and soothing. During ovulation, on the other hand, the energy is all about creation, so I'd use this time to tune into my creative powers and plan out new projects for my business or map out new content. After the first month of tuning into my monthly cycle, I looked back at things I'd manifested that month - new clients, new business opportunities and even getting published in a well-known women's magazine. What was even more interesting was how easy that month felt and how empowered I felt in myself.

The month flowed. There was no pushing myself to do things I didn't feel like doing. There was no forcing myself to create when I didn't feel inspired to do so. There was no pressure on myself to go out and socialise when all I wanted to do was curl up with a book. I honoured where I was in my cycle without putting external pressures on myself.

This ties back in with the concept of surrender. True Self Love is about surrendering to nature rather than going against it. True Self Love is about understanding that we don't need to be "on" 24/7 and that it's ok to have times of retreat and relaxation. Just as the flower doesn't bloom year-round, we don't need to either. We too must surrender to our own natural cycles and embrace the times of rest and recharge as much as our periods of growth and expansion.

A considerable part of my Self Love journey has been about inviting more ease into my life, going with the flow and tuning in to what feels good. Self Love is about allowing yourself to bloom in the exact way that nature intended and I promise you that when you embrace this way of living, you'll start to witness the most delicious manifestations show up in your life.

Dealing With Setbacks.

No rain, no flowers.

It's inevitable that as we meander through life, things won't always be rainbows and unicorns. That's life. Curveballs will be thrown at you from time to time. Negative people may cross your path. There may be moments when things you desire and have set your intentions about don't show up when you ask for them.

Yes, we can do the work on ourselves, change our beliefs, raise our vibration and practice true Self Love which will, in turn, will help us attract high vibe people, experiences and things into our life. Still, it's inevitable that along the way, there will be a few rough patches. It's important that we know how to deal with these setbacks so that we don't allow them to throw us off course.

When you start applying what you've learned in this book, you will begin to find that the "bad stuff" is less and less frequent as you are vibrating on a totally different frequency, which creates totally different experiences for you. It will almost feel like your life is so "full" of positive things (emotions, people, experience, abundance) that there simply isn't room for the negative.

Despite this, every now and then you will experience a blip. Maybe it's someone being bitchy about you, or maybe it's someone you love becoming ill or maybe even the loss of a loved one. These instances can, momentarily, throw you off course and it's important to understand how to get back on track and prevent these circumstances from derailing you completely.

Let's start with the Negative Nancy's of this world. I'm sure you know the type. We all have a Negative Nancy or a Debbie Downer in our life that thrives on misery, jealousy, resentment, bitchiness or gossip. When you embark on this journey of personal development and spiritual growth, it's natural that you will feel so passionate and excited about this work that you will want everyone to know about it. You will start to feel such powerful shifts in your energy that you'll want others to experience it too.

As you start to witness the magic unfolding before your eyes, you'll be eager for your loved ones to join the club. Sadly, not everyone is going to greet you with the same level of enthusiasm. Not everyone is going to get it. Not everyone will be ready to get on board with this work. This reminds me of a phrase from Marie Kondo's book, "The Life Changing Magic of Tidying Up." In it she writes about how to deal with messy family members who don't want you to tidy up their stuff for them. She says *"To quietly work away at disposing of your own excess is actually the best way of dealing with a family that doesn't tidy. As if drawn into your wake, they will begin weeding out the unnecessary belongings and tidying without you having to utter a single complaint. It may sound incredible, but when someone starts tidying it sets off a chain reaction."*

This is equally true of your own Self Love and Law of Attraction journey. Not everyone will get it straight away, and in fact, you may be met with a lot of eye-rolling as you harp on about Self Love, The Universe and all things manifesting. People may grumble as you offer advice or suggest books they could read. Not everyone will appreciate the power of this work or indeed be open to it. But here's the important thing: It's not your job to convince someone about the power of your mind and energy to create your beliefs or the influence The Universe has on our lives.

Your role is not to push your views on those who aren't ready to hear them. Your job is to do you in the best possible way and in doing that, you will find that the people who really need this work and will benefit from it will start to pay attention. First they may laugh, but later they'll ask you how you did it. How did you create a life so magical and full of confidence, joy, abundance and opportunities?

Now this isn't to say you can't get excited around your loved ones about your new adventure of personal growth and spiritual development. Tell them about this book, share about other amazing resources you stumble across. Just don't try and drag them along if they're not open to it. In time, if they're ready and it's right for them, they will follow.

It's so important that whoever comes into this work does so with an open mind and a certain level of curiosity and intrigue. Remember that energy flows where your focus goes and you create more of what you think about. Whatever you believe is shaping what you experience so if someone has convinced themselves that this work is a load of BS, their reality will match this. A closed mind will shut out the gifts from The Universe. You cannot expect to receive if your mind isn't open to receiving.

Now whilst it isn't your job to convince those who aren't ready to receive this work, it is your job to protect your energy from the naysayers. It's your job to make sure that the negativity of others doesn't lower your own vibration. But how? How do you protect your own energy and maintain a high vibration when you come into contact with such people?

Well, there are a few practices I love to use which I'll go into below but my simplest solution is to change the conversation and/or spend less time with these people. Just because someone is being a Negative Nancy doesn't mean you need to indulge them and engage in the conversation. Often, people use their loved ones as a sounding board for their anger, frustration, sadness and worries and I get it. Sometimes people just need to just have a rant, right? Having read this book, however, you should be well clued up on the idea that what you focus on expands. Complaining about things is simply an invitation for The Universe to send you more things to complain about.

If the loved one in question isn't aware of this, then they may not realise that "getting things off their chest" is actually doing more harm than good. Now, while you could subtly suggest that complaining isn't going to change things (before sliding them a copy of this book), as I mentioned earlier, some people won't be ready for change so the solution is to simply change the conversation.

While listening to loved ones talk about difficult issues in their life is sometimes necessary, and I'm not advocating we just shut people down completely, it's important to recognise whether the conversation is leading to a positive outcome for both parties, or creating more negativity for both parties. To offer our support and guidance to loved ones can actually feel incredibly uplifting and empowering, but only if they themselves are willing to take what we are saying on board or express thanks for our support.

When you offer someone guidance or support, and they thank you or tell you how much better it has made them feel, it makes you feel good and raises your vibration. But when you offer your support and are constantly met with "yeah but", excuses or more negativity and nothing you say seems to help, it can do the complete opposite and send your vibration into a downward spiral.

This benefits neither of you. The person doing all the venting may get a short term fix, but focusing on the negative only creates more negative. Meanwhile, you are absorbing all of this negativity without feeling like you're really able to make a difference. Issues arise when we become so over-burdened with other people's problems to the point where we feel like it's draining us. When it gets to this stage, you must prioritise who you give your time to.

Again, this isn't to say we should completely shut out loved ones who are going through a rough patch, but we do need to learn how to respect our own boundaries by saying "no". What I mean by saying "no" here is "no, I'm not open for this type of conversation, and if you're not willing to respect this, then I'm not willing to spend as much time with you."

Of course, you don't need to quite word it like this, but this should be the commitment you make to yourself. This isn't selfish. It's called Self Love. It's about preserving your energy as much as possible because if you are constantly being burdened with other people's issue to the point it drains you, that isn't going to help anyone. You don't have to go the extremes of ghosting negative friends or family members, but you should start prioritising spending time with the people who lift you up and engaging in experiences that inspire you and make you feel amazing.

As I mentioned earlier, focusing on you and your needs and doing you in the best way you can is the most effective way you can inspire others to start living their best life too. Lead by example. When you radiate Self Love, positivity and happiness, this causes a ripple effect where your positive energy has a huge impact on the energy of others. Protecting your energy is the best way you show up for those who need you in the best possible way.

If you do find yourself being an Agony Aunt for someone you care about who is going through a difficult time, one ritual you may want to put in place is called Cord Cutting.

Imagine that when you come into contact with someone, an invisible cord attaches itself between you and them. This invisible cord is like a hose through which your own energy travels. Any person you come into contact with can leave you, but the cord still remains, and energy can pass through these "hoses". If you don't cut this cord, their energy will continue to impact your own, even after you have parted ways. To prevent this, the cord needs to be cut. To do this, follow the ritual below:

The Cord Cutting Ritual

Find a quiet place where you can be alone and not disturbed. Begin by relaxing your body and taking a few deep breaths.

Once relaxed, close your eyes and call upon The Universe to help guide you through the process.

Imagine that you can fill yourself with light. In your mind's eye see a source of light above your head. See it like a brilliant star.

Imagine rays of light from this source entering into the top of your head and filling you with brilliant source energy. Breathe it in.

Imagine it completely filling you and surrounding you in a cocoon of light.

Upon feeling the presence of your guides, recite the following mantra:"Dear Universe, I call upon you to help me heal, let go, and cut any etheric cords that are no longer serving my higher purpose. I ask that all cords attached to me that are not aligned with love, abundance light and positive attention be released. Help me to release them and surround me with a healing light to protect me from future attachments. Thank You."

You may need to repeat the mantra 2-3 times. Then, you can visualise the cords being cut and as they are, you become protected by the healing light surrounding you.

You can do this as often as you need. For example, before falling asleep each night, ask yourself: "Do I have any attachments or cords with anyone that I met today?" If you find something, release it.

You can also use obsidian stones/crystals, which are very good repellents of negative energy. You can keep them in your pocket or purse, especially if you know you are going to come into contact with someone who brings a lot of drama or negative energy with them.

I also love a Salt Bath to help rid myself of the negative energies left behind after being in contact with negative people as salt has amazing cleansing abilities.

Below is an overview of this ritual.

Recipe for the Negative Energy Release Bath

Put a 'Do Not Disturb' sign on the bathroom door.

Drink a glass of water to ensure you stay hydrated and replace fluids lost through sweating.

Fill your bath with warm water. Don't make it so hot that you'll get uncomfortable.

Add 2-3 good handfuls of salt. Use a good quality unprocessed salt, such as unrefined sea salt or Himalayan crystal salt. Do not use regular table salt as this has added anti-caking agents and has been refined, which removes beneficial minerals.

The best essential oils to use for cleansing the aura are: rosemary, citronella, and eucalyptus. Lavender is a good choice, because it will also help you to relax and unwind, and is generally very safe.
Soak for about 20-30 minutes. You can assist the process by relaxing and feeling good about allowing yourself this time just for you.

Make it your intention to let go of all negativity.

You can enhance the atmosphere by lighting candles or playing relaxing music.

When complete, rinse off the salt with a quick shower if you desire, but this is not necessary.

Drink another glass of water to help your body flush out toxins.

Enjoy feeling lighter and more vibrant.

You can take a saltwater bath as often as you like, but once a week is generally enough.

I always use Himalayan crystal salt when I do a saltwater cleanse, as it is regarded as the purest salt on the earth.

It comes from ancient sea salt deposits in the Himalayan mountains and has the highest mineral content.

What To Do When Something "Bad" Happens?

A few years ago, Philip and I were out having dinner, having just celebrated an incredible month in business when I got a call from my Mum. My Dad was in the hospital. It was his heart, and he'd had to go in for emergency surgery. We immediately booked a taxi to the station to make our way up to the hospital near my parents, fear and sadness racing through me and tears drenching my cheeks. I remember seeing him lying in the Intensive Care Unit, attached to various wires, machines beeping in the background. While my Dad finally came round, this event marked the start of three months in hospital as my Dad slowly deteriorated.

This was the first time in a while that I'd really had to deal with real sorrow. In fact, it was probably the greatest amount of pain I'd ever witnessed in my life. Seeing my Dad whither away before my eyes and the Doctors not really being able to give us an answer as to what was wrong or if he'd pull through was terrifying. Seeing my Mum trying to cope with it all was even worse. While I knew I couldn't physically do anything to help the situation, by this point, I'd learned the power of my mind, and I fully believed that I could help through the power of my thoughts.

Now, I'm not claiming here to be able to create medical miracles through the power of thought, but I do fully believe that the mind has the power to help. I acknowledged my emotions and released them, but then reverted back to love and faith and allowed myself to be guided by love over fear. We were all already suffering. To dwell on our sadness and sit and cry and be angry and frustrated would mean that we were allowing ourselves to suffer even more. Instead, I knew that the best way to approach things was to find as much joy in the now, be present with my family and focus on my Dad getting better, trusting that this would be the case.

What was interesting was that during this time, I had a dramatic decrease in the amount of new client's signing up to work with me. It was almost as if business had come to a stand still, yet I felt totally at ease with this. Previously I would have allowed something like this to turn me into the victim. I would have said something like "life isn't fair," or "why me?" I would have felt like life was crashing beneath me and that nothing was going right, which in turn, would have caused more anger and frustration.

By this point in my life however, I'd done a lot of work already on my mindset and practising true Self Love and knew that I had the power to flip a negative scenario into something more powerful. This is something I invite you to do withIn your own negative situations where you feel hopeless or feel like your world is being turned upside down. Rather than asking, "Why is this happening to me?" try asking "What is this trying to teach me?", because once I did this, everything shifted. This downturn in my business was The Universe sending me a lesson. I'd been so caught up in my business I hadn't been spending as much time with my family as I knew deep down I should have been.

The slow down in my business was a gift. Less clients meant more time with my loved ones. I also truly maintain that my Dad going through what he did was also a blessing. It was the first time in a long while I'd actually spent large chunks of time with my Dad and was fully present. Thankfully, the story had a happy ending. My Dad did get better, and a heart transplant saved his life. I fully believe that our collective positivity as a family helped create the result we wanted. While modern medicine was the driving factor, I know with every inch of my being that our ability to focus on the good helped things move in the right direction.

Together, we maintained a faith that he would pull through, chose to commit to love over fear and in doing so, we witnessed miracles appear.

I firmly believe that everything we go through is also something we grow through. While it's easy to see setbacks or negative events as these terrible things that happen to us, a lot of the time these can be reframed as things that are happening for us.

True Self Love is about taking ourselves out of victimhood and acknowledging that a negative situation may actually be a lesson in disguise, an opportunity to grow or an invitation to learn something new about ourselves. As the quote says "Not all storms come to destroy you. Some come to clear your path."

Your Next Steps.

For what it's worth: It's never too late to be whoever you want to be. I hope you live a life you're proud of, and if you find you're not, I hope you have the strength to start over. ~ F. Scott Fitzgerald.

I would like to take this opportunity to say how happy and grateful I am you've not only picked up this book, but that you have also got to this page. Reaching this final chapter means that you are now equipped with a process for practising true Self Love, transforming your mindset and manifesting a life bigger than you ever imagined possible. While knowledge is power, this knowledge must, however, be put into practice if you really want to witness the magic happen. This is where the real work begins.

Reading this book once and then forgetting everything I've just shared with you is not going to create any sort of lasting change. The wisdom within these pages will only work if you implement these steps and commit to your own personal and spiritual development.

If you are serious about living by design rather than default and ready to expand into the highest version of you while creating the abundant life you are meant for, then you need to take action (albeit inspired action!) by putting the steps I've shared with you into practice.

Let's just recap what these steps are:

- Get clear on what you want and intentional about your desires. Figure out what's keeping you stuck and identify the negative beliefs that are holding you back from living your fullest potential.
- Transform those limiting beliefs and replace them with a new, more empowered set of beliefs that reflect your current reality.
- Transform your energy so that you become a vibrational match to your desires.
- Let go of negative energy and raise your vibration in order to become a magnet to positive people, things and experiences.
- Take Inspired action by doing the things that make you feel good whilst moving you closer towards your goals.
- Surrender to The Universe and trust in divine timing, knowing that your desires will arrive at exactly the moment they are meant to.
- Embrace your Feminine Energy to keep yourself in alignment, help you tap into your authentic power and help you receive your manifestations with ease and flow.

These steps shouldn't be rushed through. In fact, we take a whole three months to go through these phases within my Self Love & Spiritual Alchemy program. Doing the work can sometimes bring up a lot of unwanted junk and facing some hard truths we have perhaps been hiding away from can often feel uncomfortable. It's important to be gentle and patient with yourself through this journey.

If you're new to this, it can also feel quite overwhelming to think about all of the steps that you need to take, so let's begin by keeping things simple. A good place to start is with the morning routine I mentioned at the beginning of this book. How you start your day sets the tone for your life moving forwards, and you can use the Daily Goddess Ritual to implement parts of the Self Love & Spiritual Alchemy process. Get up early to make time for you before your day begins so that you can start your day with intention and make transforming your inner world a priority rather than an afterthought.

If you wait until the evening to do this work, chances are the day's events will have left you feeling tired and you'll push this work to one side. Ideally, you will have an hour to yourself before anything else commands your attention but if you can only commit five minutes, that's better than nothing. Let's just recap on the Daily Goddess Ritual

Meditate

Take some time to sit in silence. You can use the guided meditations within the free Self Love Club to help with this. (www.daniwatson.com/selfloveclub)

Visualize

Remind yourself of your goals and feel into your desires. As you look at the things you want to manifest, how would it feel if these were already in possession?

State Your Affirmations out loud.

Repeat your affirmations out loud and as you say the words, fully believe in what you are saying to be true.

Journal

Take some time to write out your goals and what you are grateful for. As you write out your goals, think about how it would feel if right now these goals were already in your possession.

Move

Get your Feminine Energy working and take some time to move your body without pressure on achieving a certain goal. Do some sun salutations or simply dance like no-one is watching.

Consume something that inspires you

The quality of your thoughts are determined by the quality of what you consume, so read a book or listen to a podcast that lifts you up and makes you feel amazing. Make sure to follow me @dani_watson_coaching for daily doses of wisdom.

Celery Juice

Fill your body with this green goodness every morning and watch how it transforms your energy. It's beyond the scope of this book to talk about the benefits of celery juicing, but honestly, it is amazing!

Take a Cold Shower

Get out of your comfort zone every day by spending at least thirty seconds under a cold shower. Stepping into the highest version of you requires you to get comfortable with the feeling of being uncomfortable. Taking a cold shower each morning is a great way to build up your resilience so that when you are met with situations that put you outside of your comfort zone, you can move through these experiences without them derailing you.

Creating lasting and impactful changes in how we feel and the lives we lead is about the things we do consistently. Commitment is key here. You can't expect to go to the gym once and get the body of a Victoria's Secret's model. In the same way, you can't expect to meditate once and for your life to transform overnight. Transforming your inner world so that you shape your outer world can be easy and it can be quick, but first you've got to create a little bit of forward momentum. Think of it as a snowball effect. You start with baby steps towards a small, easy to reach goal.

Choose a goal right now, which you have a relatively strong belief that it is possible for you. Once you start to witness these mini manifestations appear, you strengthen your belief that you are being supported. You begin to feel more confident in who you are and your abilities to create the life you want and from this place, things get better and better.

Starting with small goals and desires doesn't mean you are limiting yourself or settling, but you are using your smaller goals as a test to prove to yourself that this process works. So let's say you're looking to manifest a lump some of money. To begin with this could be a relatively low amount. When you are working with a smaller manifestation, it's far easier to create the belief that it is possible for you. You are much more likely to expect it to appear. Then, once you receive that money and thank The Universe for providing you with your desires, the next time round you can set your sights higher.

Sometimes, it's so easy to become focused on the huge lofty goals we forget about the smaller stuff that could equally bring us a lot of joy. While we may want to manifest millions in the bank, the dream home, the successful business or a soulmate, think of something you'd really like more of right now that feels within reach. I've manifested lots of little things along the way, things which may have not totally overhauled my life in one go, but have edged me closer and closer to the life I want. These little things have included:

A free cup of coffee from my local coffee shop.
A new business friendship.
A car-parking space right by the entrance to the shopping mall so I didn't have to walk far when it was raining.
A blog post of mine getting published on a well known site.   Getting a table reservation on the day for a restaurant that normally has a three month waiting list.
Getting an unexpected tax rebate for £250

I will often see the whole manifesting process as a fun game I'm playing with The Universe. Sometimes I'll ask myself, "what can I co-create today with The Universe?" before deciding on what I'd like more of and seeing what shows up. The quickest way to get to the bigger manifestation is to use these smaller desires as your stepping stones. Use these smaller desires as your fuel to raise your frequency and strengthen your faith in The Universe and, before you know it, things will have escalated into bigger and better things. In time, things will happen quicker, perhaps even instantaneously.

Exercise - Manifest a small gift from The Universe.

Set an intention to receive a small gift from The Universe over the next week. For example, let's say you decide to manifest a free cup of coffee. Use the Self Love & Spiritual Alchemy Process to manifest this desire.

Let The Universe know what you are asking for. Write down your desire in your daily journal. Pin a picture of this desire to your vision board.

Identify what is holding you back from having this in your possession right now? What beliefs are you holding onto that make you think you don't deserve to get something for nothing? Where are you perhaps still doubting that The Universe will support you in this desire?

Transform your beliefs to help you believe that what you want is already yours.

Create an affirmation expressing your thanks for it's arrival as if it is already in your possession. For example, "I'm so happy and grateful I have received this free cup of coffee." Create an affirmation around how you deserve to receive things for free. For example, "I deserve to receive things for free." Create an affirmation to help you strengthen your belief in The Universe. For example, "When I ask for something, The Universe always delivers"

Transform your energy so that you become a vibrational match to your desires. How would it feel if anything you wanted could show up into your life for free? Sit for a while in silence and imagine a whole 21 week where people just gave you whatever you asked for without needing to pay for it. How does that make you feel? Raise your vibration by doing the things that lift you higher. Spend time with those who bring you joy. Make space for self-care.

Take inspired action towards your desire. What can you do that maximises your chances of your desire coming into existence? Visit your local coffee, for example.

Surrender and let go. Trust that The Universe is going to deliver to you this gift at exactly the moment you are meant to receive it and it will be what you've asked for OR something better. Know that whatever you receive this week will be in your highest interests.

Rather than wondering "when is my free coffee going to appear?!", expect it to show up at any given moment and in the meantime, enjoy your life as much as possible without stressing too much about whether it will or won't show up.

Activate your Feminine Energy. Get yourself into alignment by tapping into your feminine power. To receive something for free, you have to be in the receptive mode. Ask yourself where else in your life could you allow yourself to receive a little more?

Maybe it's someone helping you in the house or with your children. Maybe it's asking for more support at work.

At the end of the week, journal what amazing things you have witnessed. Perhaps you will receive a cup of coffee. Or maybe not.

Maybe, The Universe has decided to send something even better your way. Make a note of how you feel at the end of this exercise too, because ultimately, the reason why we want to have anything is that we want to feel better.

Have you noticed a difference in how you feel through doing this exercise? What is important with this is that you have fun with this process. It's supposed to feel light and easy and enjoyable. It's just a free cup of coffee after all.

This is the beauty of starting this process with something small. There isn't too much fear around this type of desire. It doesn't feel as daunting as manifesting some of the bigger stuff. It's easy to think of the manifesting process as a fun game. It's the bigger goals that normally come with more resistance and require deeper transformations.

When it comes to manifesting some of your loftier desires, the shifts you must go through can feel uncomfortable to begin with. When there is real healing to be done, a lot of fears to work through, a lot of limiting beliefs to change and a lot of negative energy you are holding onto, the beginning of the process can feel a little bit challenging. Stick with it. On the other side of this work, you will realise that things just flow. Things are and always will be working out for you, but to begin with you may need to clear the path of a lot of junk so that you can allow things in.

Imagine yourself standing on the edge of a forest. On the other side of the forest is everything you've ever wanted; The life you want to live, the career you are passionate about, the money in the bank, the dream house, the dreamboat of a soul mate, the healthy, vibrant body. Anything you've ever wished for is there, waiting for you. From where you are right now, you can't see these things physically. You just have to trust that they are there. The only thing that is blocking your path are those trees. It's up to you to navigate your way through them.

To begin with, the trees are close together. It's dark. Sometimes you stumble. Sometimes you doubt whether you are moving in the right direction. You know however that once you get to the other side, it will all be worth it. As you continue to move through the forest, you begin to notice the trees becoming more sparse and the light beginning to creep in. Your path becomes easier to navigate, and the further you go, the lighter things become. Things begin to feel easier, and you are able to move quicker and then, seemingly out of nowhere, the forest just opens up. You have arrived.

When starting out on this path, it is sometimes difficult to see the light through the trees, but you have to have faith that what you want is waiting for you. The trees are your mindset, and once you learn how to navigate your inner world, things become easier. Then, in time, you will realise that there is absolutely nothing standing in your way. You are more powerful than what you give yourself credit for. You don't need to wait for someone to chop down the trees for you.

You've got everything you need within you right now. This process is not about becoming someone you are not, but tapping into the unique treasures within you that you didn't even realise you possess, treasures you've buried away that are just waiting to be discovered.

Confidence, self belief, resilience, worthiness, deservedness, tenacity, faith, optimism - You have all of the things within you at your disposal and, when you figure out how to unleash them, you will realise that the life you are meant for has been yours for the taking all along.

I'd like to finish with a reminder that life doesn't happen to you. It happens because of you. You have the power over what you experience. How you feel, who you allow yourself to be, what you create, the people you attract and the life that you design are up to you.

Life also is happening for you, even in the moments when you feel that it isn't the case. There is always a reason why The Universe allows things to unfold the way that they do and it will always serve your best interests in the long run. It may not make sense to begin with, but soon you will realise that every road bump you go through, you grow through and within every wrong turn, there are lessons we need to help us blossom into the women we are meant to be.

When you fully commit to this work and begin to witness all of life's little miracles along the way, miracles that you have co-created, you will realise that there are no limits in life apart from the limits we place on ourselves.

The biggest act of Self Love happens when you choose to break free of those limits.

So, my darling, I invite you now to do just that. Break free of those limits and run like wildfire towards the life you are meant for.

You are worth it.

How To Continue With This Work

If you would like to continue your Self Love & Spiritual Alchemy journey, please visit my site www.daniwatson.com for more information on my coaching program.

You can also join the Self Love Club for free by heading to www.daniwatson.com/selfloveclub. The Self Love Club is packed with free resources to support you along the way.

I'd also love to connect with you on Instagram. You can find me (please make sure to say hello!) at @dani_watson_coaching
You can also find out more about my company, The Clique, by visiting www.wearetheclique.com

Printed in Great Britain
by Amazon